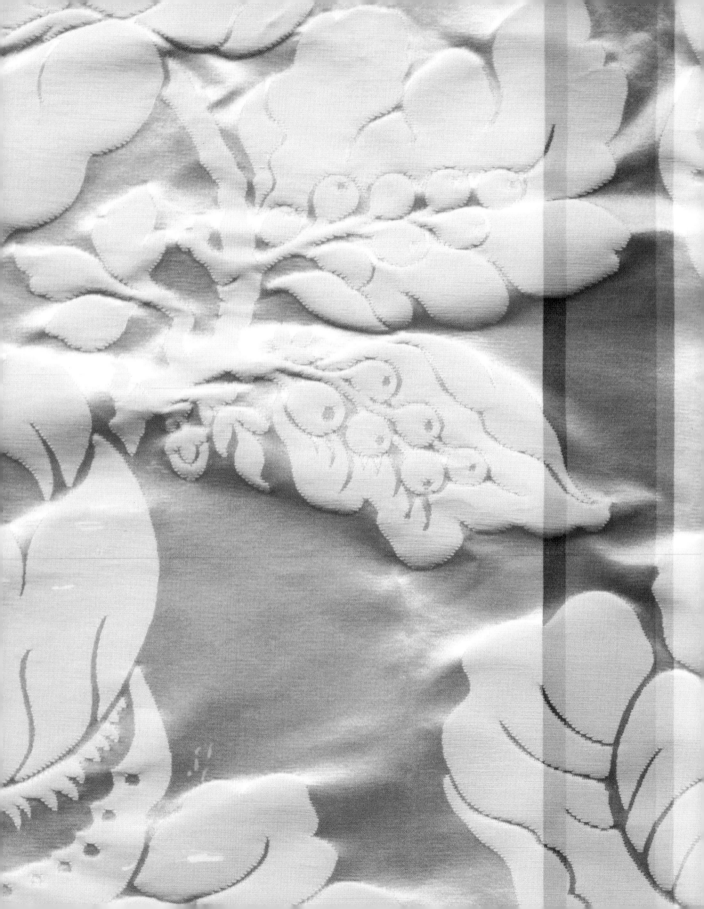

From Fibre to Fabric

Chris Halsey &
Wilhelmine van Aerssen

From Fibre to Fabric

THE ULTIMATE GUIDE TO SOFT FURNISHINGS

CLEARVIEW

CLEARVIEW

*First Published in the UK
in 2017 by*
CLEARVIEW BOOKS
22 CLARENDON GARDENS,
LONDON W9 1AZ

© *Text*
CHRIS HALSEY
WILHELMINE VAN AERSSEN
BOOKS, RIGHTS & MORE

Originally published by
HÉLÈNE LESGER BOOKS,
AMSTERDAM

*Concept, project management
and editing*
BOOKS, RIGHTS & MORE,
AMSTERDAM

First draft
CONNY VAN GELDER

English translation
LYNN RADFORD, DOETINCHEM

Photography
THÉRÈSE VAN DER LELY,
PETER KOOIJMAN A.O.

Image manipulation
STEPHAN LESGER IMAGE
MANIPULATION, AMSTERDAM

Design & lay-out
TEIN TRANIELLO,
AMSTERDAM

Production coordination
WOUTER EERTINK, GRAVEN 13,
DEVENTER

Printed in China by
LEO PAPER

ISBN 978-1908337-405

Contents

FOREWORD

For as long as I can remember, I have been obsessed and intrigued, in equal measure, by fabrics and textiles. Creating, designing and working with fabrics over the years has only served to increase my heartfelt passion for them and I consider myself fortunate indeed that my work allows me to explore the world of textiles in design and decoration with an artful aim.

It is extraordinary to think that fabric is actually one of the oldest man-made items. In fact, one can practically tell the story of civilisation through the progression and constant evolution of this seemingly everyday item. From the ancient linens and felts of early man to the complex and intricate silks and brocades of the Far East and beyond to the man-made, highly practical textures of the modern day. Each fibre and fabric conveys its own story, records a sense of time and place, depicts a culture, history and way of life simply through its very existence. How were they woven? What dyes did they use? Who made them and how? The world of textiles is vast and there are so many stories to discover and cultures to discern within this intoxicating world.

When I started Designers Guild, I was lucky to be joined in my endeavours by a young man who seemed as captivated by the world of fabrics as I was. He has of course since become a very dear friend and respected colleague – Chris Halsey. Chris and I have worked together developing collections for many years and together we have discovered many of the stories and narratives that fibres and fabrics and textures offer. He is incredibly knowledgeable in all aspects of weaving and printing and has been the resident technical expert at DG since day one.

Wilhelmine Van Aerssen has represented our brand in the Netherlands for over 30 years. Her wit and wisdom, flair and heartfelt passion for textiles are extraordinary. There is little she does not know about fabric and she is a master of decoration and interior design.

Together, they are a formidable team and I am delighted that they have joined forces and collated their many years of experience and wisdom to write this definitive homage to fibre and fabric.

INTRODUCTION

When you look at your curtains or sit on your sofa, do you understand the complex processes and techniques that have created them in all their infinite variety?

There is an indisputable magic in textiles; an incredible history stretching right back to the Ancient Egyptians and Chinese. Much has changed, but in a way nothing has changed. The original principles and techniques of spinning, weaving, dyeing and printing still hold sway today. What has of course changed is the advanced technology that has enabled faster production, more practical and durable yarns and fabrics with clever characteristics to make them easier to use and to care for.

FROM FIBRE TO FABRIC is an attempt to unravel those mysteries and hopefully give a sense of the magic that we have felt over many years in our respective roles in the industry. Much has changed in the last 50 years. When we both started our careers in the early 1960s we worked for companies that were very much the vanguard of modern textile design, but they were one of the few. Traditional fabrics were still the choice of most people in both the UK and overseas and they were mainly made from natural fibres, cotton, linen or silk. There number of magazines devoted to interior design and the home could be counted on the fingers of one hand; there were none of the TV programmes that exist today – generally speaking interior design was not considered an important area for most people. Nowadays we find dozens of magazines, TV programmes and online blogs on the subject.

Times have moved on. Whereas, back in the day, polyester was a fibre for drip-dry shirts, now it has been engineered to serve as a suitable fabric for heavy duty upholstery. Viscose is now ubiquitous in interior textiles. Dyeing and finishing techniques have advanced to give a wonderful handle to linen fabrics. With the modern day plethora of different fibres, yarns and fabrics it's no surprise that customers may be confused – even professional interior designers, retailers, curtain makers and so on can be forgiven for not understanding the complexities of the materials they are working with. As a designer or fabric retailer you need to have the knowledge to make informed choices. It's not just a question of how it looks, but also how it performs.

FROM FIBRE TO FABRIC is in many ways a distillation of all the questions and problems that we have come across over the years.

We have known each other for close to 40 years, being involved in different areas of the textile business. Between us we share an enormous amount of experience. During our long careers we have fulfilled a number of different roles in product development, marketing, technical liaison, design, colouration, interior design and decorating and sales at different levels. That experience has been gained during a period of intense change in the design, technology, production and marketing of interior textiles. Even after all this time we both admit that we learn something new every day, and hear questions we've never heard before, and we have often talked about doing a book to pass on many of the useful and helpful things we have learned along the way.

FROM FIBRE TO FABRIC is our attempt to pass on that experience to the those who wish to learn more about interior textiles, and to help those with little experience not to make expensive mistakes. We have tried to include a brief historical background for those who are interested, a layman's guide to the different fibres that go into making our fabrics and a section explaining production techniques in a straightforward way. We have also tried to point out the advantages and disadvantages of using one type of fabric rather than another and advise on care and maintenance.

The final section of the book is Wilhelmine's personal look at how to use fabrics to great effect in the home as well as issuing caveats for the unwary amateur interior decorator.

There are many images and illustrations supporting the text – we chose not only descriptive pictures showing the myriad aspects of fabrics in all their forms, but also inspiring interiors and some relevant historical reference. Much of the photography has been created specifically for the book. Also, at the end of the book we include two glossaries, one for fabrics and the other for textile terms that you may come across. There's also a guide to the care and maintenance of furnishings to help you avoid some of the common problems that can arise.

Of course, a book like this can never be completely comprehensive. New and improved yarns and new production techniques will continue to provide new design possibilities and potentially new questions will arise.

No doubt some readers may discover glaring ommissions and we could have easily made a book with at least double the number of pages. But hopefully what we have provided will enable you to make informed choices and decisions. It is always wise to ask for advice from fabric suppliers, whether it is the retail stores or the manufacturers themselves. Better to be well informed than to make an expensive mistake.

So we hope that you will gain something from our book. Our many years working with global brands whose designs are acknowledged to be the best in the world has given us a unique insight into all aspects of interior fabrics. To a large extent we have learnt as we have gone along and made many mistakes along the way, but that hasn't diminished in the slightest our passion for textiles. Every aspect of texttiles is fascinating, be it their design, their intricate production techniques , or the way they are used in interiors, whether that be a country cottage, an urban apartment, a hotel or a corporate headquarters. Textiles have an important role to fulfill, both in terms of decorating our environment and providing lasting enjoyment.

Wilhelmine van Aerssen   Chris Halsey.

PART ONE

FIBRES

ALL FABRICS HAVE THEIR OWN HISTORY AND THEIR
OWN STORY BEHIND THEM. IN ORDER TO BETTER
IDENTIFY AND PLACE DIFFERENT MATERIALS,
IT IS USEFUL TO UNDERSTAND MORE ABOUT THEIR
HISTORICAL BACKGROUND AND UNIQUE
CHARACTERISTICS, THEIR BENEFITS AND APPLICATIONS.
THIS KNOWLEDGE WILL INJECT EVEN MORE
LIFE INTO YOUR CHOICE OF FABRICS FOR
YOUR FURNITURE, CUSHIONS AND CURTAINS.

Cotton

Cotton is the most widely used fabric in the world. We wear it, we sleep between sheets made from it, and we use it in our homes. Its unique characteristics make natural cotton an ideal material, not only for clothing, but also for many interior-design applications.

Of the four original species of cotton, two come from India and Africa and the other two from South America. European explorers discovered cotton on the American continent and brought plants back with them, which led to them being introduced in Africa and India. Nowadays, cotton is produced in all the world's tropical and sub-tropical regions.

Cotton is made from the seed capsules, or 'bolls', of the cotton plant. It is a high-value crop because only around 10 per cent of the yielded weight is lost in processing. The boll, which looks like a cotton wool ball, is cleaned and combed into fibres that are then spun into yarn or thread ready for further processing. The length of the fibres largely dictates the quality of the cotton – longer fibres enable the yarn to be spun more finely. Egyptian cotton and Sea Island cotton are examples of such luxurious, and hence more expensive, cotton produced from longer fibres.

Various printed and embroidered cotton fabrics

Portrait of Marie Fargues, wife of the artist, in Turkish costume, 1756–58
Jean-Etienne Liotard, 1702-1789

History

Archaeological excavations all over the world, from Egypt to China and across the continents of North and South America, have revealed that humans have been weaving and using cotton for thousands of years. Small pieces of fabric discovered both in India and in Mexico prove that cotton fabrics were being produced as long ago as 3000 BCE, and there are indications that cotton actually dates back much further than that. Back then, India was the centre of cotton production and trade. The Old World Indus Valley Civilisation was particularly industrious in terms of spinning, weaving and dyeing cotton.

The first mention of cotton is in the Rigveda, the oldest holy book of the Hindus that was first written down around 1500 BCE. The Ancient Greek historian Herodotus wrote of Indian cotton around a thousand years later: "There are trees which grow wild there, the fruit whereof is a wool exceeding in beauty and goodness that of sheep. The natives make their clothes of this tree-wool." The German word for cotton, 'Baumwolle', still echoes this today. The English word 'cotton' and similar words in other languages is derived from the Arabic word 'qutn'.

Cotton spread through the Middle East and North Africa to the Mediterranean, reaching Europe as long ago as in the 8th century, but wool, linen and silk would remain the most plentiful textiles for many centuries. Then, in the late 16th century, France imported the first printed cotton fabrics from India. These so-called 'indiennes' became so popular that they posed a real threat to the wool and silk industry. Despite protectionist measures being introduced, the rise of cotton was unstoppable. Thanks to new inventions and

An example of an 'indienne'

improvements to spinning and weaving machinery, production speed and quality improved dramatically. James Hargreaves (1720–78), a Lancashire weaver and carpenter, invented his 'spinning jenny' in 1764 and cotton was spun by machine for the first time. The Industrial Revolution brought about tremendous changes. Europe began to produce cotton fabrics on a large scale and it soon became even more popular than silk. Checked and striped cotton was increasingly used for upholstery as well as for curtains and drapes. *Toile de Jouy*, originally produced in the French town of Jouy-en-Josas, became hugely popular. Renowned artists such as Jean-Honoré Fragonard (1732–1806) were commissioned to design patterns. Rustic, historical, mythological and oriental motifs, as well as important social themes were incorporated.

After the invention of the cotton gin in 1793 – a machine that separated cotton fibres from seeds – the US became an important cotton producer. By around 1850, the US was shipping more than a million tons of cotton to Europe each year.

At the start of the 20th century, the first synthetic fibres were developed. These were less labour-intensive, and therefore cheaper, to produce. Cotton production went into steady decline until it enjoyed a renaissance in the 1960s, largely thanks to the emergence of artificial fertilisers and pesticides. The introduction of new technologies such as plant breeding and monocultures made the cotton plant suitable for mass production. Nowadays, cotton plants are bred selectively to maximise the fibre yield of each and every plant.

The 'spinning jenny' invented by James Hargreaves

The images on a *Toile de Jouy* fabric usually tell a story, from a pastoral scene or a fable to protest against the inequality between the nobility and working classes.

The characteristics of cotton

ADVANTAGES

Cotton is strong, durable, lightweight, breathable and extremely absorbent and, importantly, relatively inexpensive to produce . It is able to withstand daylight, moisture and air well, and it can be washed and dyed.

DISADVANTAGES

Depending on the quality, cotton fabrics can crease (although less than linen), shrink and fade. Not all cotton coverings and curtain materials are machine washable, which is why many fabrics are pre-treated to repel dirt and stains and/or to reduce shrinkage, a process known as Sanforising.

Cotton and the environment

The cotton industry uses huge quantities of herbicides, artificial fertilisers and pesticides – more than one fifth of all pesticides used worldwide are linked to cotton cultivation, with inevitable consequences. By using genetic modification, the industry is attempting to reduce its reliance on chemicals – and on water, because cotton production requires large volumes of that too.

The demand for organic cotton – cotton cultivated without chemicals and only pure, organic fertiliser is growing, but it still only accounts for 0.7 per cent. Organic cotton must be picked by hand because the use of chemical defoliants is not permitted. .

Types of cotton

STANDARD COTTON (*Gossypium hirsutum*) is grown widely throughout the world, most of it in India, Pakistan, Turkey and the USA. Within this group you have various fibre lengths, which produce different qualities of fabric.

SEA ISLAND/EGYPTIAN COTTON (*Gossypium barbadense*) is an exceptionally fine, long-staple type of cotton was originally grown on Sea Island, off the coast of Georgia, USA. Varieties include American Pima cotton and the even better Egyptian variety. This type of cotton spins a much finer and smoother yarn, making it ideal for bedlinen.

THE LONGER THE FIBRE, THE FINER
THE THREAD.

Linen

No other fibre manages to combine sophistication with everyday practicality as well as linen. It is soft, strong, comfortable and durable, and – for those who like the casually crumpled look – it creases in style.

Linen is made from the woody 'bast' or fibres from the stems of the flax plant. the stems are are soaked or 'leached' to produce fibres that are then processed. Flax has very long fibres making it ideal for the production of beautiful fabrics – lace is made from the very finest yarns. The flax plant has a short growth cycle: seeds are sown in March and harvested in July. Flax grows well in many different climates, and thrives in Western Europe. Every part of the plant can be used in some form – from the seeds (linseed) to the shortest fibres. Flax processing requires relatively little water and hardly any pesticides. The production process is labour-intensive, which explains linen's relatively high price. The natural colour of linen is off-white or light brown.

History

Despite being more than 3,000 years old, the linen bandages of the mummy of the Ancient Egyptian king, Ramses II, are still in amazingly good condition. Flax is one of the oldest and strongest fibres used to make

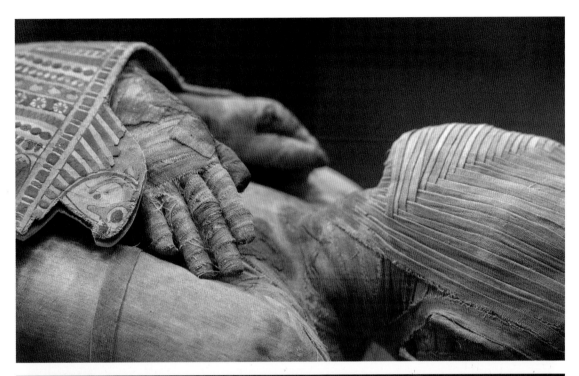

Close up of an Egyptian mummy, top, and a mummified cat, bottom, both wrapped in linen bindings.

textiles. As long ago as 6000 BCE, Flax was grown extensively in Mesopotamia and Egypt. And in Europe, traces of linseed and pieces of woven linen cloth have been found that are thought to be up to 10,000 years old. Linen was not only used for clothing. The Romans used heavy-duty linen canvas for the sails on sailing ships. Pliny the Elder (23-79 AD) wrote in the book *Naturalis Historia* of flax cultivation throughout the whole of Gallia – and he decribed Celtic inhabitants of the low countries as "weavers of linen".

The linen industry flourished in mediaeval Europe; alongside wool, it was the most widely used fibre for textiles. The countries of Flanders and Germany were important producers – the roots of the German Fugger family, which ran the largest bank and trading company in 15th and 16th-century Europe, lie in trading linen. In the late 15th century, the Netherlands was a major producer of linen damask. Linen was imported from Flanders and Silesia and originally bleached in the dunes around the city of Haarlem. The dunes were ideal because they offered lots of space and a supply of running water. The bleaching process involved the use of buttermilk, which was in plentiful supply too. Haarlem became famous for its superior-quality linen; Haarlem linen and damask bleached whiter than white were key export products for the country in the 17th century.

The Industrial Revolution, the rising popularity of cotton – which was much easier to spin and weave – and the development of synthetic fibres in the 20th century signalled the end for the linen industry. Linen faded from people's minds as it was expensive and for a while it was almost impossible to obtain pure linen. For the past century, linen has been of little significance in global textile production. However, that is starting to change. Linen has been rediscovered and, thanks to the present-day awareness of durability, is showing signs of a renaissance. Flax is once again being cultivated on a large scale in both Eastern and Western Europe and the world's best linen weavers can still be found in Ireland, Belgium, France and Italy.

View of Haarlem with Bleaching Fields, c.1650/1682
Jacob Isaackszoon van Ruisdael (1628–1682)

The characteristics of linen

ADVANTAGES

Linen is very strong – stronger than cotton, especially when wet – and lasts a long time. It is airy, breathable and very absorbent. Flax has natural antibacterial properties. Linen is soft, has a natural sheen, is easy to dye and works well in blends with other fibres such as cotton, silk, viscose and synthetic fibres such as polyester.

DISADVANTAGES

Linen shrinks more than other natural fibres. Natural scoured linen is prone to yellowing on exposure to sunlight. Linen fibres have very low elasticity. Linen crumples, even after an anti-crease treatment. Linen does not have good abrasion resistance.

Spools of linen yarns dyed
in brilliant colours

Wool

Wool is a natural animal fibre; most wool used today is obtained from sheep. There are various degrees of quality – pure new wool is wool shorn from a live sheep. Wool is often mixed with synthetic fibres, combining the best properties of both fibre types.

Wool and hair have the same chemical composition: they are both made up of proteins. A wool fibre has scales and is curly; the fibres have a high tendency to become hooked together and entangled, which makes it easy to spin. Wool has good insulating properties – it protects against the cold in a cooler climate, while desert dwellers such as Bedouins wear woollen clothing to keep them cool in the heat of the day. One of the best-known types of sheep is the Merino, a breed that originates from Asia Minor and produces soft and fine yet strong wool.

History
Humans first began to keep sheep for meat and wool around 10,000 years ago. Although wild sheep had more hair than wool, it was a couple of millennia before people started basing their decisions about which breed of sheep to keep on the quality of their fleece.

Top left: The crest of the Arte della Lana, the influential wool guild in Italy. Top right: Unspun wool.
Bottom left: Wool fabric. Bottom right: Wool carpet.

The 'wool sheep' was widespread throughout Europe by around 4000 BCE. Woollen fabrics were not only important in cold climates; the ancient Greeks and Romans wore woollen garments too. Wool felt was used for all manner of purposes, even to line soldiers' helmets in Ancient Greece.

The European textile industry thrived in the Middle Ages and wool was a source of tremendous prosperity. The best quality wool came from England – in the 15th century huge amounts of English wool were traded at major European wool markets such as the one in Antwerp, Belgium. The untreated wool was further processed in Flanders, the Netherlands and northern Italy. Much of Florence's wealth resulted from the wool trade, where it was treated, dyed and exported for many generations. Even the Medici family, who were bankers by origin, owned wool workshops and were members of the *Arte della Lana*, the influential wool guild that played a key role in the city's politics. In addition to wool cloth, broadcloth – a woollen fabric that was first woven and then milled to give a felted appearance – was another important product made in Florence. Broadcloth was warmer and more durable than simple wool cloth and was used primarily for clothing. It was rather

like the present day loden cloth, popular in Austria and southern Germany for overcoats and jackets. By the 17th century, the Dutch city of Leiden had become Europe's largest hub for wool, and had acquired an almost magical reputation. Broadcloth from Leiden had been renowned for its excellent quality and gorgeous colours since the 15th century.

The 17th century also saw the first large-scale use of wool for carpet weaving and embroidery. The very first carpets were copies of Persian and Turkish rugs, but the Europeans soon developed their own patterns and motifs. Demand for wool increased dramatically in the 18th century thanks to the introduction of new production techniques and expansion of the potential market. Woollen damask woven on mechanised jacquard looms was even able to compete on price with cotton, which was highly fashionable and very popular at that time. Australia eventually became the world's leading wool producer and continues to be so to this day. However, the demand for wool has dropped considerably, not least due to the rise of synthetic fibres since the last century.

The characteristics of wool

ADVANTAGES

Wool is breathable, it has insulating properties, and it can absorb a large amount of moisture without feeling wet. Wool fibres have scales and are curly; the fibres become hooked together and entangled making it easy to spin and mill to turn into felt. Wool has elasticity and is quick to regain its shape. Compressed wool fibre bounces back rapidly, making wool particularly suitable for interior fabrics with a pile. Woollen fabrics can be dyed to produce beautifully deep colours.

DISADVANTAGES

Wool is not particularly robust or durable, which is why it is often blended with synthetic fibres to produce strong yarns that are highly suitable for upholstery and carpets. Wool shrinks and pills, and can cause allergic reactions.

Types of wool

Although most mammals have two types of hair in their coats – 'ground' or wool hair (soft, short and fine) and 'guard' hair (hard, long and shiny) – a sheep's coat comprises only wool hairs. Any type of animal hair that feels soft and supple, and hence is similar to sheep's wool, is generically referred to as 'wool'.

SHEEP'S WOOL The most important of all the sheep breeds reared for wool are Merino and Cheviot and a hybrid that is a Merino-Cheviot cross. Merino wool is fine and soft and has a short, very curly fibre. It is milled to produce thin worsted yarns that can easily turn into felt. Cheviot, on the other hand, is a sturdy, thick wool that does not curl or 'crimp'. Cheviot fibres are much longer and shinier than Merino and the wool has a lower tendency to turn to felt. Cheviot can be spun into coarse, strong yarns.

LAMBSWOOL is obtained from the first shearing of lambs less than eight months old. This first coat is soft and supple with a particularly fine texture.

CASHMERE is obtained from the belly fur of the Kashmir goat. It is a very fine, soft hair that drapes well, which is why it is so widely used to make scarves (the fine cashmere used to make pashmina scarves is also called *pashm* or *pashmina*). It is also often blended with very fine woollen yarns. Cashmere is expensive since a this goat only produces around 150 grams of hair each year.

CAMELHAIR has even better insulating properties than sheep's wool and is also used

① Sheep ② Lamb ③ Kashmir goat

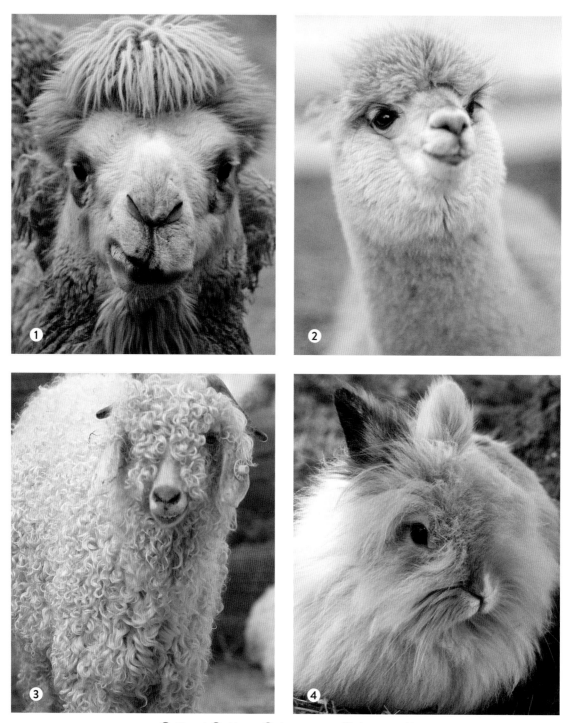

① Camel ② Alpaca ③ Angora goat ④ Angora rabbit

in woollen duvets. The wool is particularly popular because of its attractive colour, but it smells awful. The finest camelhair comes from China. White camelhair is also available, although it is very rare. Fabric known as 'camel' is usually a combination of fine wool, camelhair and mohair – it has a warm colour and deep lustre.

ALPACA is obtained from the hairs of a species of Peruvian llama called an Alpaca. The wool is shiny and its natural colour varies from brown to black. The high plains of the Andes in Peru are also home to the vicuña, a protected species of South American camelid. These animals produce Vicuña, the most precious type of hair. It is ultra-fine with a silky-soft structure and

extremely rare. The animal's coat is a natural even caramel colour so the yarn does not need to be dyed after it is spun.

MOHAIR is hair from the Angora goat. It is wonderfully soft to the touch and is the shiniest of all the wool types. Mohair is warmer and stronger than wool and is usually blended with wool, cotton, silk or polyester. The hair from young animals is used in garments whereas mohair obtained from older animals is used to produce upholstery fabrics. It makes particularly durable and high-quality velvet.

ANGORA is soft, silk-like hair that comes from the Angora rabbit.

Skein of spun and dyed wool

Silk

Luxurious, beautiful, sophisticated, elegant and sensual, silk has been one of the most coveted and valuable textiles for thousands of years. The finest silk comes from the caterpillars of the mulberry silk moth.

Silk fibre is made by the caterpillar (or worm) of the silk moth. The caterpillar spins a cocoon from two thin threads (filaments) which are coated with a naturally sticky substance (sericin). When the cocoon is completed, the larvae are humanely killed before the moth has emerged, so that the silk can be harvested. The cocoons are immersed in hot water to melt the sericin, allowing the filaments to be unravelled. Filaments are then spun together to form a thread – a process that has to be done with care as the filaments are very fragile.

Silk is relatively expensive because the production process is labour intensive and therefore costly, and the harvest is unpredictable. The quality of silk threads is dependent on climatic conditions – hot and humid conditions result in a poorer quality, whereas a warm, dry environment ensures good quality silk. The price is determined by the colour, sheen and length of the fibres.

It is well known that silk is the strongest of natural fibres. Spiders produce the strongest of all silk filaments and there are a few species that are suitable for silk cultivation, but no one has yet invented a method of producing spider silk in any great quantity.

History

The history of silk is brimming with legends going right back to the beginnings of sericulture (the cultivation of silk): Lady Hsi-Ling-Shi, wife of the Yellow Emperor, was venerated as the goddess of silk. Legend has it that one day, as she sat drinking tea under a mulberry tree, a cocoon fell into her cup. She noticed how the threads of the cocoon began to unravel in the heat of the tea, which led to her brilliant idea. The Chinese started to cultivate the silk worms, and as long ago as 4000–5000 BCE, were spinning silk and weaving it into fabrics. Other parts of the world were using

wild silk. In India wild silk has been blended with cotton since the 2nd millennium BCE Silk was worth its weight in gold and was used to pay for armies, ransoms, and taxes. Merchants brought silk to the Middle East and the Mediterranean region, and Chinese immigrants introduced sericulture into Korea and Japan. In the 6th century BCE, Greek merchants were importing Chinese and Indian silk from Asia Minor and the countries surrounding the Black Sea.

A network of caravan routes – the famous Silk Road – spanned from China to the Middle East and the Mediterranean Sea. The routes taken by the triumphal procession of Julius Caesar were bedecked with silk canopies. Although silk was highly revered by the Romans, in 14 CE citizens were prohibited from wearing silk clothing by the Senate: the 'effeminate finery of silken adornment' was deemed disgraceful.

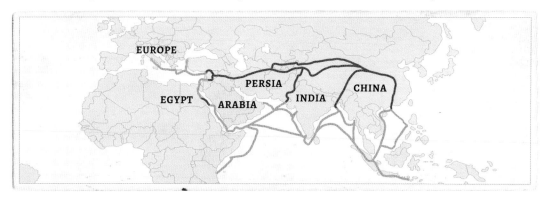

Map of the Silk Road, stretching from China to the Middle East and Europe

The Byzantines and the Arabs brought the art of sericulture to the Mediterranean Region. Africa, Spain and Sicily became important producers, and in the Po Valley, as far back as the 10th century, attempts were being made to farm silk worms, but China continued to be the largest producer of high-quality silk fabrics for a long, long time. Dyed silks, often taffeta, were made into clothing and soft furnishing fabrics and exported to Europe in large quantities. The Chinese adopted western techniques and design motifs. As long ago as the end of the 15th century, Chinese workshops were weaving, painting and embroidering textiles using European motifs, and bedspreads and wall hangings were being produced specifically for export.

Between the 14th and 16th centuries, the Italians dominated the silk trade, and developed new weaving techniques – Italian weavers were famed for their beautiful velvets. The city of Lucca had already become established as an important centre for the silk trade in the 12th century, and the weavers there were able to produce almost any type of silk fabric that was known in the Middle Ages. Genoa, Venice and Florence also became important trading centres, and raw silk was imported, mostly from the region around the Caspian Sea and Georgia. In France, Lyon was the most well known silk town. French textile producers realised the potential of the concept of 'fashion' and began creating new fabrics and costume materials for the nobility and the royal household. In the UK, beautiful, high-quality, smooth silks were being woven and English taffeta was particularly renowned – Anne of Denmark one once wore a gown made of English taffeta for the birthday of her husband, King James I of England.

The silk industry has also benefitted from the developments and improved production methods of the Industrial Revolution. However, the rise in popularity of the much cheaper cotton as well as new faster trade routes, meant that silk imported from China and Japan became cheaper. Outbreaks of diseases in the 19th century severely affected the silk worm and contributed to the decline of the European silk industry. In the 20th century, silk faced competition from new synthetic fabrics, although it continued to be a highly desirable luxury product. Today, China and Japan are the largest suppliers of silk. Italy continues to play a modest role, concentrating on luxury fabrics. The UK still produces high-quality silk fabrics, although in limited quantities.

Marchesa Brigida Spinola Doria, 1606
Peter Paul Rubens (1577–1640)

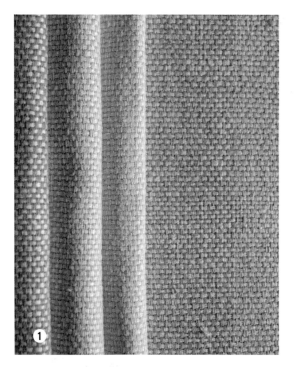

① Fabric made from tussah silk ② A yarn-dyed silk damask ③ A skein of cultivated silk on top of wild silk

The characteristics of silk

ADVANTAGES

Silk is light but strong, soft, smooth and very resilient; removing crinkles and fold lines is easy. It is warm in the winter and cool in the summer. Silk can absorb a lot of moisture, quickly; it does not create static and is rarely affected by mildew or moth damage. The enormous absorption capacity of silk also means dyes take very well, producing fantastic colours.

DISADVANTAGES

Silk is sensitive to heat and sunlight and can discolour and fade. Cheaper silks are particularly fragile. A good-quality silk can last for years – even centuries, but is expensive.

Types of silk

WILD SILK comes from the caterpillars of moths that live in the wild rather than the cultivated mulberry silk moth. The cocoon of a wild silk worm has a coarse golden yellow thread with an irregular structure. Wild silk is thicker and slightly less pliant than cultivated silk, the filaments are not as glossy and it is more difficult to dye. Fabric made using wild silk creases more easily and tends to shed more fibres.

CULTIVATED SILK is made from the cocoons of the farmed mulberry moth and caterpillar – *Bombyx mori*. This species is native to Europe and China and lives on the leaves of the mulberry tree, which is why cultivated silk is also sometimes called mulberry silk. The caterpillar takes about three days to spin its cocoon, and produces a very fine thread between 1,000 and 1,500 metres long. From this, a length of unbroken thread can be unravelled (reeled), which consequently produces the best quality silk. What remains of the cocoon is also processed - even the shortest fibres can be used.

RAW SILK is made from any silk thread that has not had the sericin – the natural gum layer that forms a protective layer around the fibres – removed. Raw silk is not glossy, but is the strongest and most durable silk, and another forte is its beautiful structure. Although raw silk may be dyed, colours tend not to be absorbed evenly into the fibres and so the material is often left undyed. Raw silk should never be washed in hot water or the sericin will melt and the texture and handle of the fabric will become limp and floppy.

SILK DAMASK is a jacquard-weave fabric made with silk. Originating in China, this weaving style was the predecessor of brocade. The name comes from the Syrian capital Damascus, which for centuries, was a crossroads for the trade routes between the East and the West.

SILK TAFFETA is a light, usually shiny, smooth, plain weave fabric that has a characteristic rustling sound when it moves. It is often woven with contrasting colours in warp and weft to give the characteristic changeant or 'shot' appearance.

DUPION SILK is produced using 100 per cent wild silk for the weft threads. It is made using the fibres from a double cocoon (from a male and a female caterpillar) where the threads have become intertwined. The resulting fabric has a slightly slubby texture and is stripy in character, giving an elegant effect. It can be used for curtains and occasional upholstery such as small chairs or cushions. It is not strong enough to use for general upholstery.

TUSSAH SILK is is another silk made with wild silk thread. It is usually beige or brown.

Dupion silk

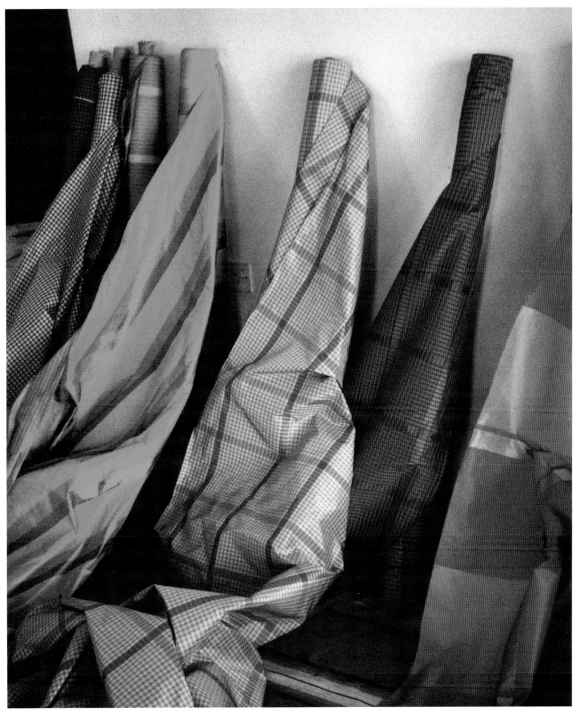

Rolls of silk taffeta

ARTIFICIAL SILK

Viscose (also called rayon viscose) was one of the first man-made artificial silks, and it continues to be one of the most important fibres today. It is famed for its high lustre.

The raw material for viscose production is chemically modified plant cellulose. Most of the raw material is wood pulp from specially cultivated coniferous trees or the remnants of cotton linter. The cellulose is treated with chemicals to produce a syrupy substance that is then forced through a spinneret, like a shower head with microscopic holes. The end result is a very fine, potentially endless thread that can be spun into yarns. Viscose has a very high sheen, but this can be modified by adding a variety of chemical substances such as matting agents and dyes to the viscous fluid – even the structure of the fibre itself can be altered. Generally, the filament is chopped into shorter fibres that can then be spun into a yarn in much the same way as cotton fibres are spun.

Viscose is relatively inexpensive and can be mixed with other fibres including cotton, linen and synthetics. It is a very versatile fibre and can be used for everything from simple cotton-blend fabrics to sumptuous velvets. In furnishing fabrics it is often utilised to give particular threads a shiny effect.

New developments mean that it can be produced in a more environmentally friendly way, by processes that use less water and power. Moreover, there are new yarns that are stronger, easier to care for, crease resistant, easier to clean and are less damaging to the environment. Nowadays, bamboo, maize stalks, and even proteins such as milk, soya and sea algae can be used as the raw material.

History

As early as the 17th century, it was suggested by an English biologist that it must be possible to make artificial silk. In 1889, after years of research, Hilaire Bernigaud (1839–1924), the Count of Chardonnet, succeeded in producing the first artificial silk by accident. The French silk industry had suffered greatly as a result of an epidemic that was affecting silk worms and Bernigaud had gone in search of a remedy; a chance chemical spill in his darkroom produced an alternative yarn. Although beautiful, the yarn was extremely flammable and was therefore unsuitable. In 1894, English chemists developed a better method and called the resulting fibre viscose.

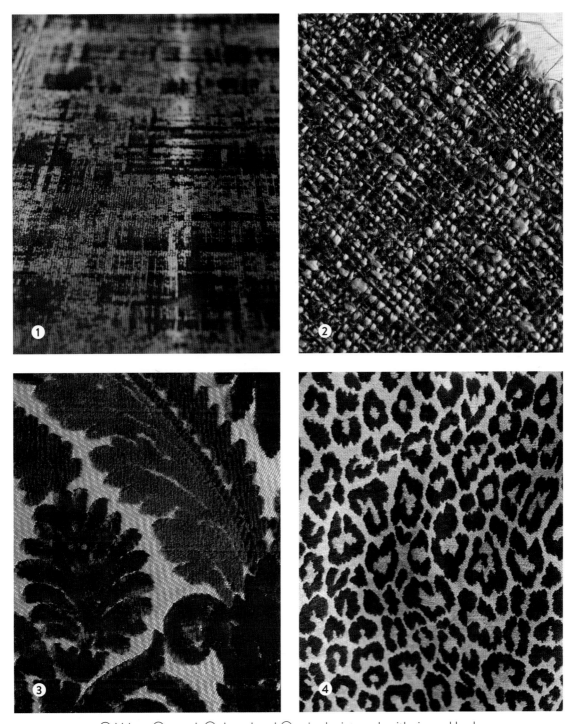

① Velvet, ② tweed, ③ damask and ④ animal print, made with viscose blends

Characteristics of viscose

ADVANTAGES

Viscose is soft and supple; it feels like silk and has a beautiful sheen. The fibre can be made into any desired thickness or length. Viscose absorbs moisture quickly and easily, even more so than cotton. It can be washed at high temperatures but needs a cool iron.

DISADVANTAGES

Viscose is not particularly strong and creases easily, which is why it is often blended with other fibres. It is weaker and less hard wearing than cotton and is prone to mildew: it is susceptible to damage if stored in damp conditions. Because of its hygroscopic nature it is prone to dimensional instability as it reacts with atmospheric moisture.

Other types

ACETATE is more elastic and creases less than viscose. The fabric absorbs little moisture and as such, dries quickly after washing. It is similar in appearance to silk and is often used for textiles where it makes a suitable alternative to silk in taffeta constructions, typically for fabrics with a moiré effect.

LYOCELL and TENCEL are completely recyclable and biodegradable. They are strong, hardly shrink, can be dyed easily and feel soft to the touch.

MODAL is a viscose yarn with improved properties made from reconstituted cellulose.

CUPRO, also known as Bemberg is a particularly fine viscose, often used in high-quality jacquard velvets where its lustre and handle is akin to silk velvet.

An embroidered silk and viscose blend

Figured velvet with bemberg pile

Synthetic fibres

A world without synthetic fibres is now almost unimaginable, even though synthetic fibres are a relatively recent development. Nylon came to market in 1938, and alongside polyester is the most commonly used synthetic fibre in the world.

The raw material of synthetic fibres is petroleum. In the refinery, the crude oil is separated into a number of constituent parts that are then further processed. By the addition of chemicals such as acid and alcohol, new substances are formed – granules, powder and sometimes liquid slurry – that are extruded under pressure through a spinneret with minuscule holes to form thin, very long filaments. These filaments cool and solidify and are spun together to form a thread. By changing the shape of the holes in the spinneret, certain characteristics can be altered in the fibres. The fibre's resistance to wear can be increased for example, and the structure of the fibre itself can be changed in a number of ways too to make it smooth, woolly, matt, glossy and so on.

By mixing a natural fibre with a synthetic thread, the unique properties of both materials are combined and you will get, for example, a stronger fabric that is less likely to shrink.

History

The success story of the synthetic fibre began in the US with the discovery of nylon by Wallace Carothers. For many years, scientists had been searching for an artificial fibre that could emulate the natural characteristics of animal and plant fibres. Carothers specialised in polymers – large molecules with specific structures - a new field of study about which little was known. He was given free rein by the US chemical company, Du Pont, to carry out research, and developed nylon, a material that was very similar to silk (and a name which according to tradition is a combination 'N'ew 'Y'ork and 'Lon'don). It was a great success and in 1941 resulted in the most exciting innovation in the fashion world, the nylon stocking.

During the World War II, the production of nylon was requisitioned in its entirety by the US government, and was used for making, amongst other things, parachutes. Meanwhile, research continued and the rise of the synthetic fibre became unstoppable. In the UK and Germany, large research projects were in progress and in the UK in 1941, polyester was developed, followed swiftly by acrylic in 1942. In the 1960s manufacturing techniques had improved so much that it was possible to influence the properties of the fibres themselves, and much work was carried out on improving flame retardant properties for example. Nowadays, the emphasis is on innovation, and the number and variety of synthetic fibres is astounding. Microfibres made of a polyester nylon blend are currently the thinnest, lightest fibres – a roll of thread 10 kilometres long weighs a mere 30 grams – and the advances continue.

Synthetic fibres and the environment

Even though much consideration is given to the improvement of production processes, the petrochemical industry continues to be highly polluting. Under the right conditions, plant and animal fibres will break down, and after a period of time will have been completely reabsorbed into nature. However, the petroleum-based synthetic fibres can last up to 200 years before they decompose on the rubbish heap. For this reason, the raw materials are recycled and research into alternatives is underway. PLA (polylactic acid) is a bio-plastic, a synthetic plant fibre that can be extracted from maize, sugar cane, sugar beet and potatoes. The thread has been on the market since 2002 and has proved to produce a good, useable material for clothing and soft furnishings. Research is also being carried out into the possibilities of using yeasts, bacteria and moulds.

Characteristics of synthetic fibres

ADVANTAGES

Synthetic threads are light and very strong; they are highly elastic and very hard wearing. The threads also have a good resistance to moth damage and mildew, and absorb little moisture. The fabrics are usually easy to maintain, easy to clean, and cheaper than natural fibres.

DISADVANTAGES

The yarns are not always as beautiful as natural fibres, and can attract dirt more quickly and have a tendency to pill. The production of the fibres is harmful to the environment.

Types of synthetic fibre

ACRYLICS, also known as polyacrylics, are soft, airy fibres with good insulating properties. They absorb little moisture, which is why they can feel 'sticky' when worn as clothing, and are therefore more suitable for knits. They are easy to care for, dry quickly, and hardly crease. Acrylics can be blended with wool, cotton or viscose and are used for imitation fur and soft furnishing textiles.

ELASTANE also known as Lycra, is an elastic fibre that does not shrink, holds its shape and is easy to wash, so is often used for (sports) clothing and underwear. Lycra can be woven in with a stable thread such as cotton or linen so that the unique properties of that fabric can be combined with the elasticity of Lycra.

LUREX is usually a tape thread made of synthetic yarn coated with a thin layer of aluminium, but can also be produced from synthetic fibres. The addition of dye pigments creates Lurex in a wide range of colours.

MODACRYLIC is a light polyacrylic fibre with good flame-retardant properties when combined with cotton or linen. It is soft and warm, strong, does not crease, dries quickly, and holds its shape. Modacrylic is used in combination with cotton or polyester for curtains, upholstery, and fabrics that are intended for outdoor use. Amongst other things, it is used to make synthetic or 'Polar' fleece and incredibly realistic imitation fur. One disadvantage is that it has a tendency to pill.

POLYAMIDE In the synthetic fibre industry, research into how to improve the properties of synthetic yarns is intensive. Polyamide is one example whereby its static properties have been greatly improved along with its resistance to dirt. After polyester, polyamide is the most

Spools of lurex yarns and examples of fabrics woven with synthetic yarns

important man-made fibre. It is light, strong and crease resistant; it is durable, moisture resistant and easy to care for. Polyamide does tend to pill however.

POLYPROPYLENE (PP) is the lightest textile fibre, and will float on water. Polypropylene absorbs virtually no moisture, dries extremely quickly, can be recycled, and is strong. It is often used to make ropes and cables and has replaced jute and sisal amongst others, for this purpose. Because it is light and weather resistant, polypropylene is often found in sports clothing. Soft polypropylene yarns can be blended with other fibres for use in soft furnishings, such as carpet backing fabrics, carpet yarns, wall coverings and upholstery textiles. One disadvantage of polypropylene is that it produces static.

POLYESTER is an improved version of nylon, it is strong and flexible, water repellent and crease resistant, so holds its shape. Second only to cotton, it is the most commonly used fibre for textiles and is usually blended with linen, wool or cotton. Polyester has a high resistance to UV light, which means colours stay 'fast' for longer. It is suitable for use in most soft furnishings as it is easy to wash, can be dry-cleaned and is easy to maintain. One disadvantage is that polyester can pill.

TREVIRA CS is a branded high-quality polyester fibre that has excellent flame-retardant properties. As a result of much development over the last 20 years, it has many of the most desirable qualities of natural fabrics and is often used in public spaces, hotels, restaurants and for office furniture.

Man-made vs Synthetic

There is a common misunderstanding between what are generally known as man-made fibres and those called synthetic. There is no complicated mystery here. Man-made fibres are those that use natural substances, normally plant cellulose, processed to form a liquid paste, which is then forced through a spinneret that looks like a shower head with its fine nozzles. The liquid mix solidifies as it is extruded and forms a filament. Examples of this are viscose, cupro and acetate. They may be used as filament yarn, but more typically will be cut into short fibres and spun in much the same way as cotton.

In furnishings the most common man-made fibre is viscose and its derivatives. It is produced mainly from wood pulp and other naturally occurring cellulose materials such as bamboo. It is produced in a wide range of filament thicknesses from the fineness of silk up to heavier counts more akin to wool. Chemical or mechanical manipulation of the basic material, can provide additional desirable features such as enhanced lustre and improved wet strength. It is very suitable for combining with other fibres like linen or cotton to give the properties of both yarns to a fabric.

In contrast synthetic yarns are made from raw materials such as petroleum or coal tar. They break into a number of broad groups, but all are based on long chain polymers with varying characteristics. The main groups are: Nylon (polyamide); Polyesters such as Terylene, Trevira CS or Dacron; Acrylics such as Dralon or Courtelle; Elastomerics such as Lycra and Modacrylics such as Kanekaron and Lufnen.

Most man-made fibre types were developed in the early to mid 20th century and were attempts to replicate the properties of the main natural fibres. Hence acrylic was a substitute for wool, polyester for cotton, rayon for silk. The intention was that the new fibres would have all the appeal of their natural counterparts but would be easier and cheaper to produce and not rely on the vagaries of climate for their production. Alas, they fell rather short of the visual appeal and comfort of the natural fibres.

However, through continuous development and refinement in recent decades, huge improvements have been made in the appearance, feel and care characteristics of these synthetic fibres and the fabrics that employ them.

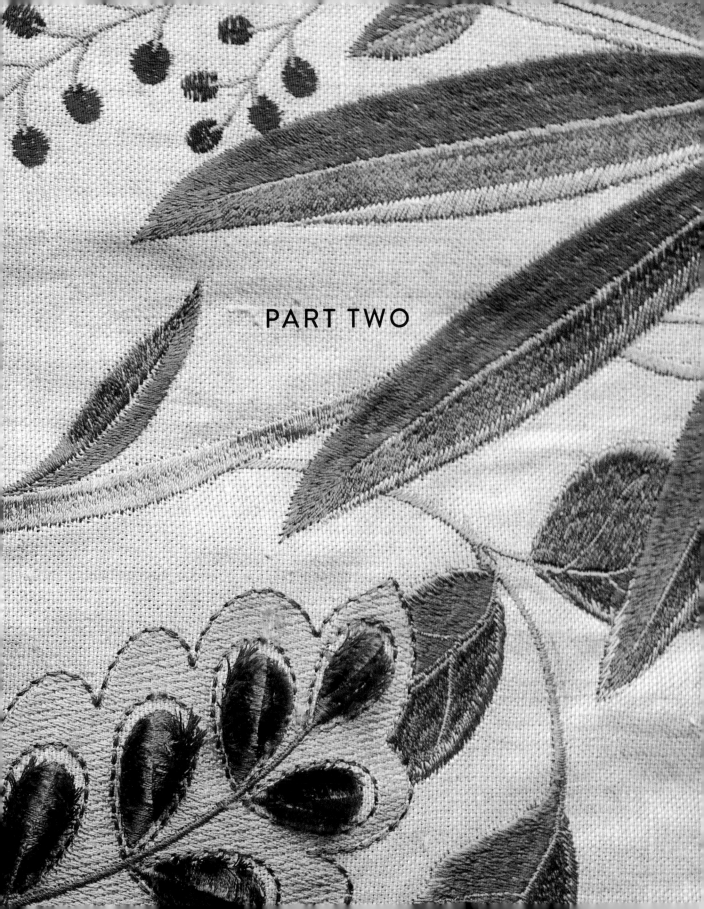

PART TWO

FROM FIBRES TO FABRIC

THERE IS AN INDISPUTABLE MAGIC
IN TEXTILES; AN INCREDIBLE HISTORY
STRETCHING BACK TO THE ANCIENT
EGYPTIANS AND CHINESE, THROUGH
THE ENSUING MILLENNIA
TO THE PRESENT DAY.

From Fibre
to Yarn

Much has changed in the way fabrics are made, but in a way nothing has changed. The original principles and techniques of spinning, weaving, dyeing and printing still hold sway today. What has changed is the technology, which has enabled faster production, more practical and durable yarns and fabrics with clever characteristics that make them easier to use and to care for.

Yet visit any of the great textile museums or archives and you will realise that there is nothing new. Indeed, many of the ancient artisanal techniques created highly complex and incredibly beautiful cloths. The industrial age in the 19th century, and the technological age in the 20th and 21st centuries, may have permitted high speed production techniques, but it has largely lost the qualities and complexity of the most extravagant and beautiful hand made textiles of the past.

History

No one knows precisely how and when humans began began making yarns– perhaps with a rock and a thin strip of leather. Most experts agree that spinning was invented more than 10,000 years ago in the Middle East, although some claim it may even date back some 15,000 to 20,000 years.

La Fileuse, 1873
William-Adolphe Bouguereau (1825–1905)

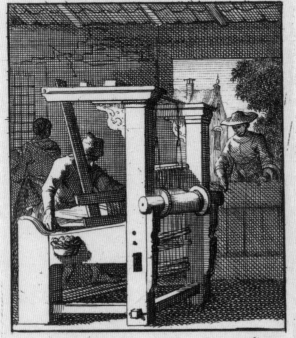

The Weaver, 1694
Caspar Luyken
(1672–1708), after Jan
Luyken (1649–1712)
One of 100 engravings
depicting professions,
made by Caspar and
Jan Luyken called
'The Human Trade'

A shuttle from a mechanised loom, which like the spinning jenny, was developed
during the Industrial Revolution.

For many thousands of years, all the yarn used – whether to make clothing, curtains and carpets or ropes and sails for ships – was spun using a spindle (a cylindrical rod featuring a flat disc to act as a weight) and a distaff (a tool for holding wool or flax). The hand spinning wheel was invented somewhere between 500 and 1000 CE in India and reached Europe in the Middle Ages. This represented a tremendous improvement since it enabled more yarn to be spun, and more quickly. Flanders and France, both important wool-producing regions, were quick to adopt the new technique. One of the first images of a woman spinning wool with a spinning wheel can be seen in the illustrated papal decrees of Pope Gregory IX dating from the early 14th century. The Saxon spinning wheel introduced around 1530 featured a foot pedal, thus leaving both hands free.

The textile industry played a key role in the Industrial Revolution. It was an era of invention and change. As the population grew, spinners and weavers struggled to keep pace with the growing demand, especially for cotton fabrics. The shuttle was developed, as was the spinning jenny – the world's first spinning machine. The production process was continually mechanised, ultimately resulting in mass production and the modern factory system.

Nowadays, the entire process has become automated, from spinning to weaving. The focus is on quality and on developing yarns and fabrics with their own unique characteristics. Another more recent yet important challenge for the textile industry is to develop manufacturing processes which comply with stringent health and safety and environmental requirements.

Spun yarns and filament yarns

A distinction is made between two types of yarns: spun and filament yarns:

SPUN YARNS are made up of relatively short fibres (also known as staple fibres) that have been entwined or spun. These yarns are never completely smooth since the ends of the fibres protrude. Spun yarns are usually made from natural raw materials such as flax, cotton or wool. But they can also be jute, hemp, nettle, ramie, sisal or raffia. The resulting fabrics are generally more voluminous, offer better heat insulation and moisture absorption, and feel softer than synthetic fabrics.

The only exception in this group is silk, which is a naturally occurring filament yarn. Only the poorest quality silk yarn, usually from damaged cocoons is converted into spun yarn.

FILAMENT YARNS are synthetic yarns that are made up of endlessly long threads (filaments). The yarns are smooth since they have no fibre ends. Fabrics produced using synthetic yarns tend to be thinner, smoother and have a more even appearance. They are usually strong fabrics that shrink very little, if at all.

Nowadays, synthetic spun yarns are also available. These are made by cutting the filament into shorter fibres and spinning in a similar way to cotton or viscose. It is possible to combine the best properties of both types by blending natural fibre yarns with filament yarns.

Spinning yarns: twisting or doubling

SPINNING is the intertwining loose fibres or filaments to form a yarn. Different devices are used to turn different types of fibres into a yarn, but the principle or each remains the same. In a spinning mill, the fibre mass is first opened up, mixed and cleaned. The fibres are then spaced out evenly and spun to form a yarn.

TWISTING is the process of intertwining the fibres, or filaments. This ensures the fibres hold together and gives the yarn the right degree of strength.

DOUBLING is the process of twisting at least two yarns together to form a thicker and stronger thread. Twisting and doubling can be done in two directions: left (S twist) or right (Z twist). The twist direction influences the fabric's ultimate appearance – think of the distinctive lines in a twill fabric, for instance. A blended yarn is a combination of yarns of different colours or textures or of different fibres.

The quality of the yarn depends on various factors, including the length of the fibre used to spin it. Cotton that has been spun from very long fibres is fine, strong and usually more expensive, whereas cotton made from a short fibre is cheaper, but also weaker. Fabrics produced from fibres that are too short sometimes have the tendency to pill. The number of twists per centimetre is also important. Yarn with a high number of twists is much stronger and more robust than yarn that has only been given a low twist. The number of twists also affects the yarn's texture and therefore how it feels to the touch.

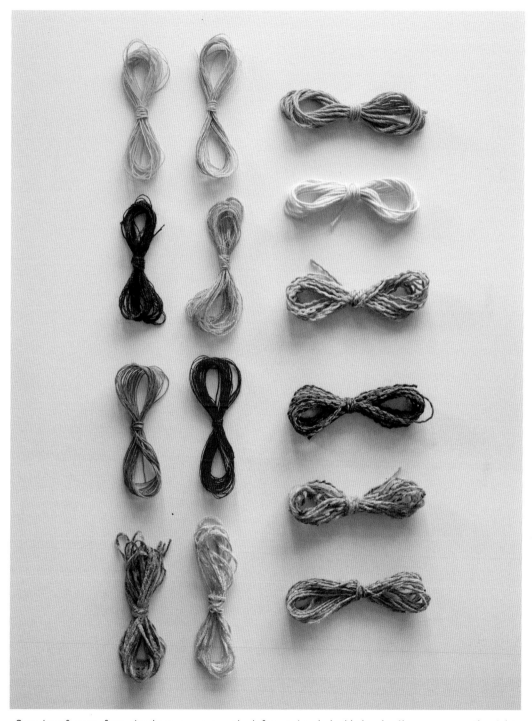

Samples of yarns, from simple spun yarns on the left to twisted, doubled and mélange yarns on the right

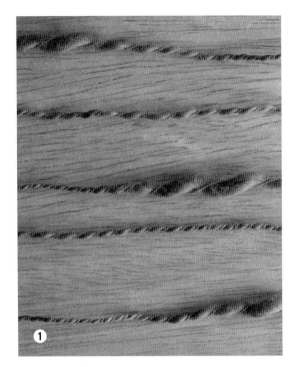
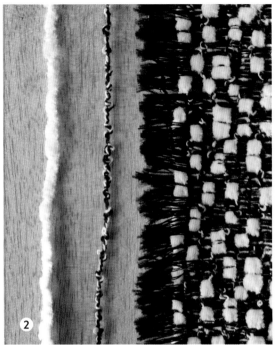

① Slub yarn ② Chenille yarn ③ Silk filament yarn

Yarn variations

Yarns which have a different texture or colour to standard yarns are called fancy yarns. Fancy yarns are made in various ways.

YARNS WITH TWIST EFFECTS

These are made by combining different types and/or colours of yarns. Twist effects can also be created by feeding the yarns into the spinning process at different speeds. The number of twists per metre can also vary greatly.

- *Slack twist yarn* has very few twists, which gives the yarn extra volume. These yarns are used to produce knitwear, blankets or towels.
- *Regular twist yarn* has enough twists to hold the fibres together and gives the yarn sufficient strength. Regular twist produces yarn that can be used for many different fabrics.
- *Voile yarn* is a special hard-twist yarn that results in more strength and robustness. Voile yarn is used to produce fine, sheer curtain fabrics, for example.
- *Crêpe twist yarn* is twisted so tightly that the yarn starts to curl. This is used to produce crêpe fabrics.

YARNS WITH SPUN EFFECTS

Fancy yarns with spun effects are produced by changing the fibre composition during the spinning process.

- *Mélange yarn* comprises a combination of differently coloured and/or irregularly coloured fibres.
- *Slub yarn* imitates the look of silk or linen. Some sections of the slub yarn are purposefully spun to be thicker than others.
- *Bouclé yarn* is a novelty yarn with a looped effect. This is created by feeding the decorative yarns in at varying speeds.
- *Boutonné* is a yarn with knots and thicker sections that are created by wrapping the foundation yarn around the effect yarn, or vice versa, intermittently.
- *Space-dyed yarn* is a yarn that is dyed at intervals with different colours to create an effect in the finished weave structure.

OTHER YARNS

- *Two-ply yarn* is twisted evenly from two yarns.
- *Cable yarn* is the result of intertwining two or more ply yarns to create a rope-like effect.
- *Chenille yarn* has fibre ends protruding from it on all sides and derives its name from the French word for 'caterpillar'.

From yarn to fabric

Humans have been producing textiles for many thousands of years. Materials, colours and processes have changed over time, and tastes and trends have become increasingly influential. However, the way fabrics are made remains unaltered. We still weave and knit , except that nowadays it is not done by hand, but using ever-more advanced machinery.

Modern airjet looms run 10 times faster than the old shuttle looms, although they cannot weave the incredibly fine silk jacquards of yesteryear as the yarns are too fragile to withstand the demands of high speed production. Of course, fine filament polyester or acetate is more than strong enough, but they do not have the inimitable lustre and handle of a pure silk.

Whether made from spun or filament yarns, twisted or plied, elastic or bulky, from ultra-fine to ultra-coarse, or novelty yarns made from flax, cotton, wool, silk, wood or oil, one thing is for sure: there is a huge variety available.

Weaving and knitting (tricot) are two different ways of intertwining threads together to make fabric. There are other means of creating fabrics such as felting, knitting or lace making, but these are rarely used for furnishing fabrics.

Weaving is done machines called looms, on which horizontal threads (the weft) are passed on a shuttle between vertical threads (the warp) that move up and down alternately. In

Handloom

Preparing the warp yarns prior to weaving

modern-day weaving machines, the shuttle has been replaced by small projectiles, (rapiers) or compressed air or water jets. These techniques are much faster and less noisy than earlier looms. In principle, woven fabrics are almost always more or less rigid, unless they contain lycra to add stretch.

The knitting process forms interconnected loops using one or more threads (either by hand using knitting needles or by machine). In contrast to most woven fabrics, knitted fabric is elastic and can be stretched. Most tricot fabrics are knitted on either flat or circular knitting machines. By using various techniques and many different types of yarn, it is possible to produce a broad spectrum of fabrics with a wide range of different characteristics and properties.

Weaving

Put very simply weaving is the method of producing fabric by the interlacing of one set of lengthwise yarns (the warp) with a second set of widthwise yarns (the weft). There are many complexities available to the weaver.

Woven fabrics are produced on a loom on which the warp threads are raised and lowered by various means to allow the insertion of the weft yarns to create the fabric. The way in which the warp and weft yarns interlace is what creates the weave structure, from the very simplest plain-weave cottons right through to the most complex brocades, damasks and brocatelles. The raising and lowering of the warp threads and the insertion of the weft in different sequences is what creates the variety of weave structures and associated patterning possibilities.

The simplest looms can weave plains, satins and twills and many variations of these. Small repeating patterns can be woven on dobby looms where groups of warp yarns can be raised and lowered to create small motifs. Larger scale, more complex patterns need to be woven on jacquard looms where it is possible to manipulate even individual warp yarns.

Traditionally the weft was carried across the loom in a shuttle, and still is today for hand-loom fabrics and some specialized fabrics where weaving speed is not the primary concern. It is also the preferred method for delicate fabrics where high speed looms might cause yarns to break. Over the last 50 years the need for faster and more economical production has lead to the introduction of more and more sophisticated means of weft yarn transport.

Rapier looms are amongst the most common in use today as they are very versatile. They do not use shuttles, but carry the weft by means of small pincers on the end of flexible rapiers that pick up the weft thread and carry it halfway across the loom, where another rapier picks it up and pulls it the rest of the way.

For really high-speed production the simpler weaves airjet looms are preferred. These are looms in which the weft yarns are carried across the loom by a series of air jets.

Weaves

The weave construction describes the way in which the warp and the weft threads cross during the weaving process. This can be done in many different ways, and it largely determines the resulting fabric's appearance and properties. Other influential factors include the yarn's type and thickness, its twist or ply, its colour and any subsequent treatments.

The quality and the suppleness of a fabric depends on its density, or the number of threads per square centimetre of fabric.

There are three fundamental or elementary types of weave – *plain weave, twill weave* and *satin weave*. These three weaves enable the majority of all fabrics to be produced. Each elementary weave has several variations derived from it. The most complex fabric designs can be made by varying the thickness, type and colour of the warp and weft threads.

PLAIN WEAVE

With a plain-weave fabric, the weft thread goes over one and under one, hence it is also known as the one-up-one-down method. This is the oldest, simplest and most common way of weaving. The warp and the weft play a roughly equal part in the resulting cloth. Plain-weave fabrics look the same on both sides, so there is little difference between the right and wrong side of the fabric.

Thanks to the yarns crossing one another multiple times, the weave is relatively strong and the cloth (the weave) does not usually produce lint. It is primarily used for thin fabrics and is less suitable for producing heavy cloths since they tend to be too stiff. Examples of plain-weave fabrics include sheeting cotton, batiste, muslin, poplin, taffeta and crêpe. Panama weave is a variation on plain weave in which the warp and the weft are each made up of two yarns. The fabric has a higher density and is therefore stronger. Canvas is an example of Panama weave. Half Panama is a

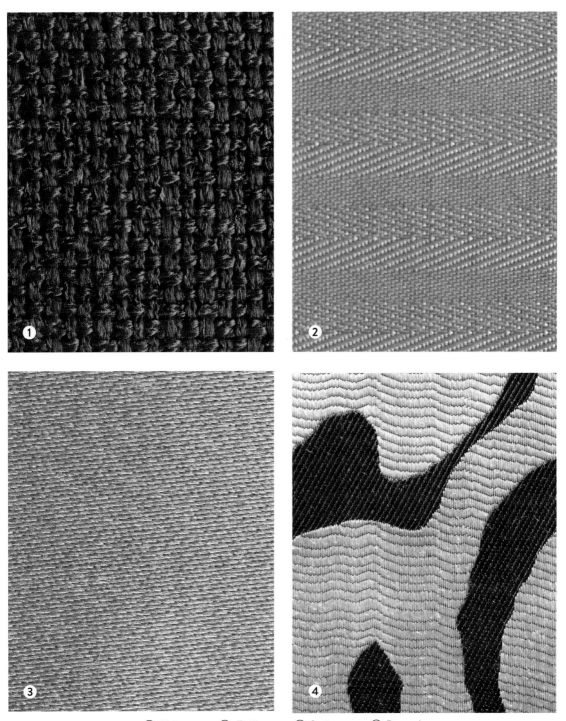

① Plain weave ② Twill weave ③ Satin weave ④ Damask

fabric in which double yarns in one direction are crossed with single yarns in the other direction.

TWILL WEAVE

With fabrics made using twill weave , the weft thread passes over one and under two. Each subsequent weft thread is offset, which creates the distinctive diagonal lines known as twill lines or 'wales'. The diagonal lines can run from bottom left to top right or vice versa – they are knwn as left and right twills. There are many different types of twill weaves including double twills, warp twills, weft twills, zigzag twills, diagonal twills and reinforced twills. The twill weave is particularly suitable for heavy cloths such as denim: a warp twill whereby thin, very densely set warp yarns are combined with less densely set, yet thicker, weft yarns. In contrast to plain-weave fabrics, twill cloths tend not to be printed. Rather, they are dyed in plain colours or have patterns woven into them. Scottish tartan is a double twill that is the same on both sides. Other examples of twill weaves include gabardine, herringbone, serge, denim, tweed, flannel and peach skin fabric.

SATIN WEAVE

 A satin fabric has warp yarns that 'float' over a number of weft yarns. This creates a the typically lustrous appearance because light is more easily reflected from the surface. Depending on the number of weft yarns that the warp floats over they are known as 3-and-1, 4-and-1 or sometimes 5-and-1 satins. The binding points (where the threads cross) are offset from one another. The warp yarns are usually finer than the weft and very closely set. There is an alternative version, often called weft satin or sateen, in which the weft threads rather than the warp yarns float.

Satin weave creates fabrics with a very supple handle and which drape well. However, due to the large proportion of 'floating' threads, the fabric is much less durable than plain weave, so is more suited to curtains, bedcovers and cushions than to upholstery.

Damask is a patterned jacquard fabric in satin weave. Combining the warp and weft satin and plain weave creates matt patterns on a lustrous background to create its characteristic contrasting effect.

Different yarns, different weaves

Fabrics can be decorated and embellished in a wide variety of ways. In addition to the countless weaving techniques, all manner of different yarns, fibres, colours and treatments can be used.

COLOURED YARNS

Coloured yarns offer plenty of creative choice. Whether for stripes, blocks, checks, dots, floral patterns or images, colour can be used with any type of elementary weave. It is possible to combine yarns in different colours – for the warp or weft or both – or to use printed or space-dyed yarns. Geometric patterns such as pied-de-poule, houndstooth or gingham check are usually woven in dobby weave. For non-geometric patterns such as floral designs, alternating satin weaves are used, and are woven on jacquard looms.

YARNS OF VARYING THICKNESSES

Ridges and textured effects can be created using yarns of varying thicknesses. Alternating thick and thin warp or weft threads in a particular sequence create a certain texture. By combining thin, densely set yarns for the warp with thick yarns for the weft or vice versa, it is possible to produce a clear horizontal or vertical ribs. Examples of fabric with ribs are repp, ottoman, taffeta and poplin.

A COMBINATION OF DIFFERENT YARNS

Changeant or 'shot' taffeta is one example of a fabric made using different yarns: the warp is often filament acetate and the weft viscose. Lamé and brocade feature a warp of silk or a synthetic filament combined with a weft of metallic yarn or lurex. The fabric can be produced in a plain weave, dobby weave or jacquard weave.

SPECIAL YARNS

Crinkle-look fabrics are woven using yarns that shrink differentially, so that the yarns that do not shrink cockle slightly to give a seersucker or crumpled effect.

Seersucker is made using a combination of smooth and shrunk yarns to produce alternating wrinkled stripes and smooth stripes.

Crêpe fabrics are woven with tightly twisted yarns to create their distinctive granular surface. Crêpe fabrics can also be woven in what is known as granité weave. In this case, the binding points are spread randomly across the cloth to produce fabric with an irregular, slightly bumpy texture.

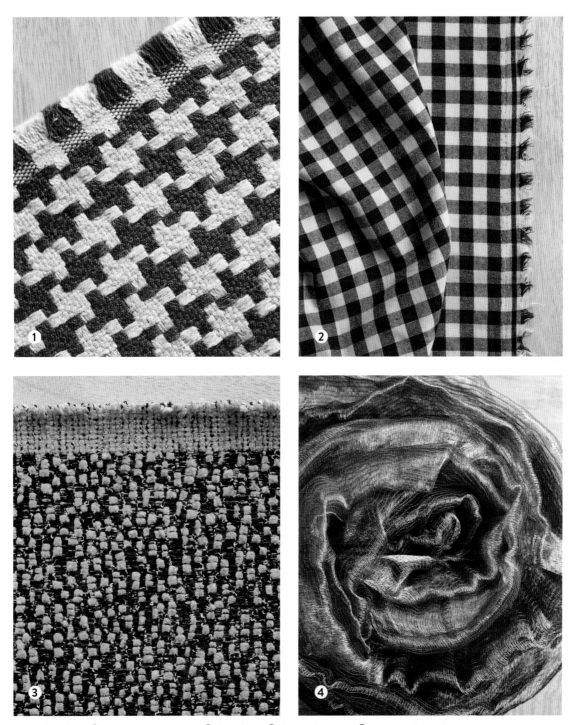

① Houndstooth fabric ② Gingham ③ Chenille fabric ④ Voile with metallic yarns

PATTERNS

We have always been surrounded by pattern. No matter where you look, they are just waiting to be noticed – specks of sunlight on a wall, stars in the night sky, a balcony's railings, a honeycomb structure or the neat arrangement of a flower's petals. Patterns capture our imagination, which is why we decorate our clothes, homes and possessions with stripes, dots, checks, swirls, flowers, birds, leaves and so on.

The line and the circle are two of the oldest shapes known. Fascinating cave paintings by our prehistoric forefathers featured geometric shapes and objects. A simple line became a zigzag, a rectangle, a diamond or a triangle. A circle became a dot, and dots could be joined together by lines to form a star. The shapes and patterns became increasingly complex, and ultimately resulted in the inspiring works of art that we still enjoy to this day – from the impressive geometry of the Moorish mosaics or the striking ribbing on a vaulted Gothic ceiling to intricate embroidery and gorgeous woven fabrics.

The history of patterns

For centuries, fabrics were dyed, woven and embroidered by hand, or printed using hand-made stencils and blocks fashioned from clay, wood or metal. Patterns were repeated, sometimes being printed on top of each other in different colours to create complex, multicoloured designs. All the resulting fabrics had one thing in common: imperfections. The motifs were positioned by sight, which often resulted in irregular gaps between them and misaligned joins when patterns overlapped slightly. This all changed with the onset of industrialisation and the introduction of automated manufacturing processes, and these in turn opened up possibilities for new patterns. The 18th century saw the emergence of more intricate patterns printed using steel and copper rollers, such as *Toile de Jouy*, and today's state-of-the-art techniques make spectacular photo-realistic effects possible.

It is easy to spot the difference between hand-woven fabrics and machine-woven ones. The latter are much more evenly woven, which has made it possible to design increasingly complex patterns. With hand-woven fabrics, the weaver had (and still has) some freedom to incorporate his or her own ideas, even when replicating an existing or traditional pattern. Nowadays, such imperfections are regarded as a key part of the charm and exclusivity of a hand-woven fabric.

Example of a Chinoiserie pattern

Patterns have been important throughout history, and echoes of the same patterns can be found all over the world – from colourfully striped cloth from Ghana to the characteristically subtle stripes of the Gustavian style. And some patterns will forever be associated with a certain country, like tartan and Scotland.

Trade routes such as the world-famous Silk Road had a huge impact on how patterns developed – the rise of brocades and damask fabrics that reached Europe in the Middle Ages, for instance, and the immense popularity of Chinoiserie during the Rococo period. Artistic movements have also played an influential role, especially more recently. Styles such as Cubism, Bauhaus and the Bloomsbury Group and artists such as William Morris, Sonia Delaunay – widely regarded as the 'inventor' of abstract patterns on textiles – Raoul Dufy and Matisse have all left their mark.

 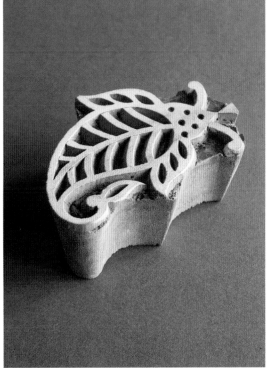

The carving of a woodblock for printing a paisley pattern and a finished block

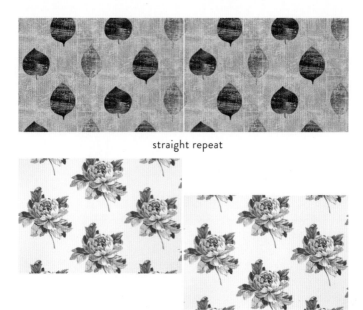

straight repeat

half-drop repeat

Pattern repeats

All patterned fabrics are made up from individual motifs (simple or complex), which are repeated vertically and horizontally. With furnishing fabrics it is essential that the pattern matches at the edges so that when lengths are sewn together to make curtains, blinds, bedcovers or upholstery the pattern runs continuously across the join.

The repeat of a design can be constructed in a number of different ways, the two most common being straight repeat and half-drop repeat. This is a subject that causes much confusion even amongst professionals, but it is important to understand that the designation 'straight' or 'half drop' is significant only in relation to what happens at the edges of the fabric and dictates how it can be joined. Fabric that has a straight match can be joined quite straightforwardly, whereas fabrics with a half drop repeat require more care, both when estimating the quantity required and when cutting the curtain lengths. In simple terms, with half drop repeats you need extra fabric in order to match the pattern on the joins as the matching point is 'half dropped', so an extra quantity equivalent to half of the repeat size needs to be added.

Types of patterns

A pattern is a design comprising one or more images, shapes or elements which are repeated horizontally and vertically. A single element – a line, a dot or a flower – called a MOTIF forms the basis of a pattern. The way in which the motifs are arranged is called the REPEAT. Different types of repeat include straight, half drop, offset.

Patterns can be divided into four main groups: GEOMETRIC or GRAPHIC PATTERNS, FLORAL PATTERNS, PICTORIAL PATTERNS and ETHNIC PATTERNS. Many different words can be used to describe the patterns, such as 'romantic' for tiny flowers, 'subtle' for a motif that is hardly discernible, or 'bold' for geometric patterns.

Large-scale patterns are generally used for interior design and upholstery fabrics. The layout is carefully considered so that rolls of wallpaper or curtain fabrics can be joined together without interrupting the pattern. Smaller, more random patterns are mainly used for clothing, but breaking with such guidelines and conventions can often produce surprising effects! Over the years, the names of certain fabrics have become synonymous for patterns. The word 'chintz' probably immediately brings to mind an English country-cottage look featuring a large floral pattern, yet chintz is actually a fabric of Indian origin with a surface gloss.

An machine can embroider up to 8 metres at a time, but each colour must be added separately. A design can have up to 8 colours, so it's a time consuming process.

There are two distinct types of patterns: WOVEN PATTERNS, whereby the fabric itself forms the pattern, such as with damask, Scottish tartan or striped satin. The warp and weft threads are dyed beforehand or woven or tied in a certain way to create textures and colour effects. Meanwhile, an applied or SURFACE PATTERN is the name given not only to printed or embroidered fabrics, but also to tie-dyeing in which bindings are applied to the warp and/or weft threads before weaving so that they are only partially dyed and batik, where the pattern is applied directly to the fabric by molten wax, which is removed again after the dyeing process.

① Geometric or graphic pattern ② Floral pattern ③ Pictorial pattern ④ Ethnic pattern

Moiré

A moiré fabric is one in which a wavy
pattern is created on the fabric, producing
a watery, iridescent effect. Traditionally
it was created in an weaver's studio,
largely by hand, by passing the folded
fabric under tension across variously
configured wooden 'combs'. Ideally the
fabric would have been silk to impart the
requisite lustre. What is important is the
weave structure, which should be of a fine
ottoman or horizontal rib. The effect is not
permanent as it results from the manual
distortion of the weave, which creates
differential reflection and it reduces or
disappears completely over time as a result
of wear-and-tear or laundering.

Nowadays permanent moirés are available
that are made by embossing a polyester
base fabric that is then heat set, using
rollers with an engraved moiré pattern.
To the purist this is never acceptable as
a regular repeating pattern is evident,
whereas with the traditional method the
pattern is more or less random. Sadly there
are now very few craftsmen capable of
working in the traditional way, and they
are mostly in and around Lyon, France.

Colour

In 1856, 18-year-old British chemist William Perkin (1838–1907) discovered the first synthetic dye by accident while conducting an experiment, and it made him rich. The colour, mauve, became a huge success in London and Paris when Queen Victoria wore a dress with a mauve velvet train to her daughter's wedding. More synthetic colours rapidly followed, in striking shades of crimson red, violet, blue and green. Up until then the palette of available colours had been limited to natural dyes obtained from plants, minerals, shellfish and certain insects.

Two of the most important plant-based colourings were indigo (blue) and madder (mostly red). Indigo is one of the oldest dyes around – it was used by many ancient civilisations, from China to Mesopotamia and Peru. Most indigo came from India (the name 'indigo' originates from the Greek word *indikos* which means 'Indian') and reached Europe via the Middle East and the Mediterranean region. Back then, indigo was still a luxury product; in Europe, fabrics were dyed blue using woad, which contained only very small amounts of indigo. From the 16th century onwards, woad was replaced by indigo that was being imported from Asia along the new trade routes by sea.

The madder plant originally comes from Asia Minor and the Eastern Mediterranean, but from the late Middle Ages onwards it was also grown in large quantities in the Dutch regions of Zeeland and South Holland. The red dye became known as Turkey red or rose madder. In order to dye cotton or linen using madder, the fabric first had to be treated with a metal salt. The resulting colour depended on which metal salt was used, and could be anything from bright red to lilac or violet – or even black.

The colours indigo, madder and mauve

Sir William Henry Perkin, 1906
Sir Arthur Stockdale Cope (1857–1940)

Dyeing and printing

A fabric can of course be woven using differently coloured yarns, but it is also possible to add colour to the cloth by dyeing or printing it. For optimum results, the basic material should be as white as possible, which is why textiles are usually scoured and bleached before being dyed.

DYEING FABRICS

The fabric, the fibres or the yarns are placed in a dye bath to allow the dyestuffs to penetrate deep into the fibres. Different fibres require different dyes and treatments. In the case of synthetic yarns, a colour is added during the production process. This method is called solution dyeing.

PRINTING FABRICS

Surface decoration on fabric has been carried out for millennia using many different methods. Originally it would have been by hand painting, then by various means of resist dyeing such as batik or tie-dye. Woodblock printing developed in China before 200 CE during the Han dynasty and the earliest known fragments are of a floral pattern printed on silk. Stencil printing was developed to a high degree of sophistication in Japan and Indonesia.

Block printing was not found in Europe until the early 15th century when it was used both for printing text on paper and for stamping patterns on leather or fabric. The technique is both slow and labour intensive. As the technique developed over the next few centuries increasingly complex multicoloured designs necessitated the use of dozens of blocks, all carved by hand using blocks made from fruitwood.

The slow speed of block printing made it expensive and in the late 18th century the much faster technique of roller printing was developed in the UK. Unlike block printing though, roller printing employed an intaglio method whereby the pattern was incised into a metal roller and released to the fabric under pressure. This was a much more complex technique but it meant that up to 10,000 yards of fabric to be printed in a 10-hour shift.

In the 20th century screen printing was developed, originally by flat screens, but more recently by rotary screen, now the main method employed. Screen printing is simply a development of stencil printing and allows more detailed patterns and multicoloured designs to be printed. In flatbed printing a fine synthetic mesh is stretched across the frame;

A bath for dyeing hanks of yarn

The build-up of pattern and colour in printing.
Each individual layer of colour is printed on top of another.

in rotary screen printing the cylinder itself is composed of a fine mesh of nickel. The mesh is then coated with a photosensitive emulsion over which the design is fixed, then exposed to light. The areas of emulsion that were exposed will harden, and the remaining areas can be washed off, creating what is essentially a stencil. Colour is then squeezed through the screen by means of a squeegee blade onto the cloth. Modern screen printing machines, both flatbed and rotary, are able to print up to 24 colours, and can print up to 1,000 metres of fabric an hour.

The newest development is digital printing, using machines similar in technology to desktop inkjet printers, which allow the printing of a limitless colour palette and large pattern repeats. The pattern is only limited by the size of the computer files, although patterns of up to 3 metres high are perfectly feasible. This method is currently much slower than screen printing, the fastest machines capable of up to 150–200 metres of fabric an hour and the smaller machines can only print up to 30 metres of fabric per hour.

A digital printing machine uses a similar technique to a desktop inkjet printer.

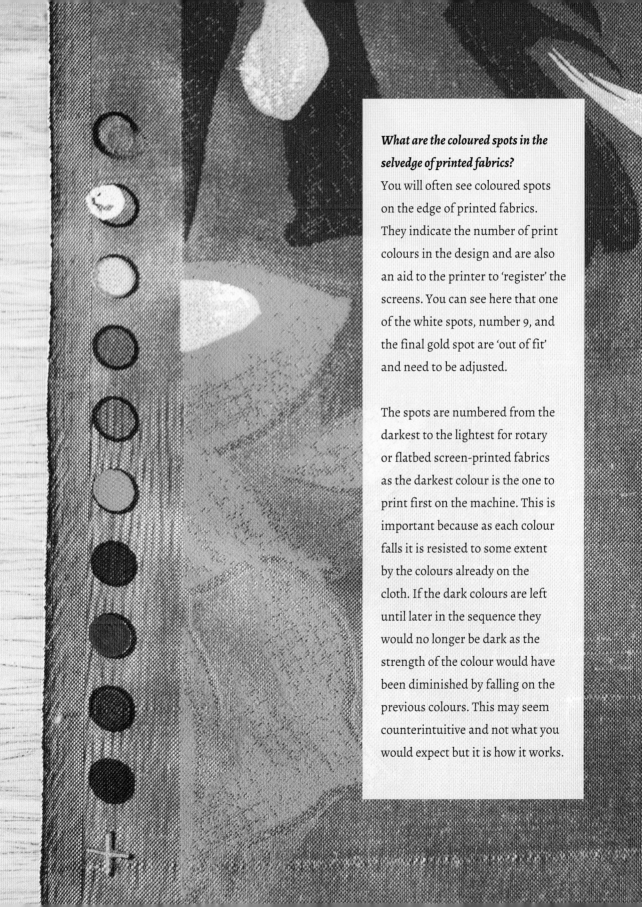

What are the coloured spots in the selvedge of printed fabrics?

You will often see coloured spots on the edge of printed fabrics. They indicate the number of print colours in the design and are also an aid to the printer to 'register' the screens. You can see here that one of the white spots, number 9, and the final gold spot are 'out of fit' and need to be adjusted.

The spots are numbered from the darkest to the lightest for rotary or flatbed screen-printed fabrics as the darkest colour is the one to print first on the machine. This is important because as each colour falls it is resisted to some extent by the colours already on the cloth. If the dark colours are left until later in the sequence they would no longer be dark as the strength of the colour would have been diminished by falling on the previous colours. This may seem counterintuitive and not what you would expect but it is how it works.

Fabric treatment

Nowadays, we make high demands of our home furnishings. Curtains and upholstery fabrics are required to be stylish, colour fast, dirt repellent and flame retardant, 'Finishing', also known as treating, chemical finishing or dressing, gives a fabric a certain appearance and adds – or eliminates – certain properties. Fabrics can be finished in many different ways, and a distinction is made between visible and invisible finishes.

VISIBLE FINISHES

These are processes that change a fabric's outward appearance and add value to it in some way. After weaving, the upstanding fibre ends protruding from the fabric are removed by singeing or shearing. Another way of lending a fabric a smoother finish is to press it between rollers under high pressure – this is known as calendering. Synthetic resin is often used to give cotton fabrics such as chintz a long-lasting glazed, or chintz, finish.

Giving fabrics a raised surface makes them warmer, softer and more voluminous, plus it improves absorbency. The fibre ends are lifted slightly using small, sharp teeth. In the case of milling, the woollen fabric is either entirely or partially turned into felt; the wool fibre scales are matted together creating a thicker and stronger cloth. Tweed and flannel are examples of this kind of treatment. Other finishing techniques include glazing, pleating, embossing, PVC coating and backcoating.

INVISIBLE FINISHES

These are processes that give the fabric special properties to make it easier to use or care for. The fibres, yarns or cloth are treated with chemicals or synthetic resin that cannot usually be seen on the surface of the fabric. Examples of such finishes include anti-static, crease-resistant (non-iron or self-iron), or water-repellent and stain-repellent characteristics. Textiles used for interiors are subject to increasingly stringent flame-retardant requirements. 'Flame retardant' means ensuring that a fabric is slow burning and self-extinguishing. Trevira CS is polyester with a flame-retardant content, and modacrylic also has good flame-resistant properties, particularly when mixed with other fibres such as cotton or linen. Textiles can additionally be treated with a mould resistant finish – particularly important for furniture that stands outside for much of the year.

The birth of a collection

It is hard for many of us to remember the design climate prevailing in the 1960s and early 1970s. At that time there was little in the way of contemporary fabric design although some leaders were ploughing a new furrow, making use of the undoubted talent coming from art schools like the Royal College of Art. Several UK companies spring to mind as typifying this new, fresh approach. Heals Textiles, headed up by the formidable Tom Worthington were in the vanguard, producing designs by the likes of Lucienne Day and Barbara Brown; Hull Traders, a small brand whose main designer was Shirley Craven also were at the forefront. Edinburgh Weavers produced wonderful jacquard weaves designed by notable artists of the period such as Graham Sutherland and John Piper. Also leading the way, and very much an influence, were the Scandinavian brands such as Danasco, Marimekko and Unika Vaev, as well as Falconetto in Italy.

Also very much a household name and influence at that time was Sanderson whose traditional florals have reached truly a global market, and whose advertising campaigns were among the earliest in this field. Let's not forget too that for many people the traditional look was what was

required and many brands were at the forefront of that look, and still are. The likes of Colefax and Fowler and Jean Monro in the UK, Rubelli in Italy, Brunschwig & Fils in New York and Nobilis, Pierre Frey and Braquenié in France were masters of that particular art.

So although the world of interiors has changed enormously over the last few decades it is still very different from the world of fashion, although there are nevertheless more and more similarities today than was the case before. In earlier years, before interiors were considered an important design element by many people, textile producers might bring out just a few designs each year. Now new collections are launched in Spring/Summer and Autumn/Winter just as in the world of fashion. In both worlds, designers determine which patterns, colours and textures will influence the look in the seasons ahead. But just how exactly is a new collection put together?

The story begins at least a year or two before the launch. The designers start to make initial concepts inspired by a wide variety of sources, ranging from fashion trends, foreign travel and nature to more abstract sources such as photography, film and architecture. And that's leaving aside the incredibly rich and diverse history of pattern making that plays such an influential role. Whatever the source of inspiration, in the studio the design team considers how best to translate their ideas into actual designs, and whether they will be more suitable for the summer or winter collection.

Then come the first sketches: the sources of inspiration are transformed into workable patterns. Nothing is set in stone at this point. All manner of suggestions are made for the use of colour and pattern, and there is plenty of experimentation with the scale of the designs and different layouts. Since confidentiality is crucial at this stage, the only people allowed access to the studio are the designers and their teams. There then follows a lengthy process of editing the designers' work to create a coherent collection of designs that reflects the company's handwriting.

A key part of this process is the decision about which kind of cloth (for example, linen, silk or cotton) the pattern will be printed on. Designers and product development teams can choose from dozens of different fabrics and, since each type will have its own unique effect on the overall look and feel, this is a very important moment. Consideration must also be given to the performance characteristics of different cloths – are they more suited to curtains and blinds, or could they be used for upholstery and loose covers? Price is clearly something to be considered as well, as there needs to be a realistic and commercial price level for customers.

This is also when the team needs to decide which manufacturers to work with – once again, each supplier has their own particular printing methods and techniques, strengths and weaknesses. Once the final selection of designs has been made the painted artworks are passed to specialist engraving studios who will make the colour separations to enable printing screens to be engraved. This is an immensely skilled process and whilst it is true that nowadays laser scanning and CAD (computer aided design) software make automatic colour separations possible, if you really want to see every nuance of shading and fine detail there is no substitute for painstaking tracing work.

There follows yet another stage in the process – the engraver's proofs need to be checked and fine details corrected. During this time the design studio create a range of colourways to be sampled. Then together with the printer's design manager and senior colourist, the optimum print programme and machine set-up are determined for each design. The printer then produces trial samples, which rarely – if ever – offer exactly the desired outcome first time. The colours are subsequently re-mixed and fine-tuned until the results are perfect. The designers and product development team spend hours and hours liaising with the engraver and printer in order to fine tune designs and colours.

Then, the final stage. The company's senior designers and product developers visit the printworks to supervise production printing. At this point there are many fine adjustments that can be made to machine setup and colouration so that the final result accords as closely as possible with the designer's original concept. This can be a time-consuming process as the first sample from the machine still needs those final adjustments to be made. Also when using the best-quality vat dyes the fabric needs to pass through a giant machine to fix the colours in the cloth to prevent subsequent fading. It would be unusual to be able to print more than two or three colourways in a day, especially when many designs contain up to 20 different colours, all of which may need altering to achieve the final perfect result.

In parallel with the design process, the collections must be evaluated from a financial perspective. A new collection needs to be financially viable since it involves a huge level of investment. Therefore, the production costs of a collection are calculated very carefully as they must accord with sales forecasts.

Don't forget, what we have described above is the design process for just one design. To fill a sample book, and hence to be able to present a complete collection, countless fabrics, patterns and colour combinations must be designed and evaluated. It is not unusual for a colourist to have to mix up to 500 different shades for a print collection. Furthermore, since the designs are often produced by a number of different manufacturers, careful planning is essential. Therefore, it is hardly surprising that so much time elapses between the designer's initial ideas and the presentation of a new collection in its entirety.

In the world of fashion, new designs are shown on the catwalk in order to judge response before a metre of fabric is produced, or a single garment cut and sewn. For interior collections hundreds of meters of fabric has to be produced before a single metre of it has been sold! Fabric is needed to make sample books, to cover chairs and sofas and to make cushions, curtains and even lampshades for initial advertising and point-of-sale photography so that retailers and consumers can see examples of possible uses for the fabrics.

Once the sample books and the promotional materials are ready, the time has come to launch the collection. This is usually done during an event, often a textile trade show such as *Maison&Objet* in Paris, at which all the new fabrics are presented and the background to the new collection is explained. For major interiors companies, introducing a new collection means a launch in up to 80 countries at the same time. Media coverage is very important in order to introduce the a collection to consumers and to show them how the fabrics could look in their own interiors. Therefore, to support retailers, the brand's PR department works closely with local agents and distributors to promote the collection to interior design magazines and newspapers in each market.

PART THREE

USING FABRICS
IN THE HOME

FABRICS OFFER US A QUICK AND EASY WAY
TO ALTER AN INTERIOR'S AMBIENCE.
THEY ARE KEY TO CREATING ATMOSPHERE,
WHICH CAN IN TURN HAVE A SIGNIFICANT
INFLUENCE ON OUR MOOD – SOMETHING
WE OFTEN TEND TO FORGET.

Curtains

There are many reasons for choosing to include curtains in an interior; they not only add style and atmosphere to a room, but also muffle sound, provide privacy, offer extra insulation and so can even help to save energy.

Curtains can be a welcome and decorative addition to your home. It is important to carefully consider which fabrics are right for the room in question, and to enlist expert advice if you are in any doubt. Opt for quality and get the curtains made by a competent professional, since even the most exquisite fabrics can lose their allure in the wrong hands. Another point to remember: curtains can be seen not only from the inside, but also from the outside.

Medieval interior with four-poster bed, c.1420
From *Les Très Belles Heures de Notre Dame du Jean de Berry*

HISTORY

Originally, rather than being hung in front of windows, curtains were hung around a bed or were used to separate off part of the living area. The very first bed curtains were little more than simple pieces of cloth hung from beams in the ceiling. In the Middle Ages, people began to pay more attention to beds, and added a loose canopy above. By the end of the 14th century, these had evolved into four-poster beds and the entire bed was decorated with intricately embroidered fabrics and beautiful drapes. This protected people while they slept – not only against the cold, dust and dirt, but also from insects or creatures that might fall from gaps in the ceiling, not to mention from prying eyes – privacy was virtually unheard of until well into the 19th century. The length of the drapes held a clue to the owner's status: only the highest members of the nobility were able to cover their four-poster beds entirely; lower ranks had to make do with less fabric.

For many centuries, the bed was one of the most expensive items in a house. In fact, the most ornate bed was often not even slept in, but was instead a display piece and the focal point of the house.

In many countries, most families lived in a single room, sharing everything including the bed, which was often little more than a cupboard built into the wall. Only the nobility and the wealthiest families had their own separate sleeping quarters, and even then they shared the space with their servants. The 'bedroom' did not emerge in its own right until the second half of the 15th century. The bed also played a key ceremonial role: back then, the invitation to share a bed represented a huge political honour. The method of covering the bed became increasingly more lavish, intricate and extravagant, reaching a peak during the reign of Louis XIV (1638-1715). Known as the 'Sun King', he introduced a strict protocol in his royal court and organised various stately matters from his bed. The elite – men and women alike – followed the King's example and received visitors and business partners in richly upholstered four-poster beds. It was a way of displaying their wealth, taste and sense of style to the world. Hence, while curtains continued to have a practical functional, they were also used as a status symbol.

From the 17th century onwards, houses increasingly had glass windows, and the use of curtains moved to the windows. As well as allowing daylight to flood in, the glass also meant that people could see inside, so the windows were partially covered by lightweight, transparent fabrics or blinds. Thick curtains were not added until the 18th century, and even then they were considerably simpler than the extravagant bed curtains that had been so popular a century earlier. One new development was the Austrian blind, also known as the festoon blind or ruched blind, which was originally made of unlined silk and hung flat against the window.

Crying woman looking out of the window, 1865
Willem Steelink Sr (1826–1913) after Diederik Jamin

In the 19th century, the Industrial Revolution brought about tremendous changes. Mass production of household textiles and the later development of synthetic dyes and colourings had a major impact on the style and colours of curtain fabrics. Curtains made from lace evolved into what we now know as net curtains or voile, for instance. The growing bourgeoisie with ever-more money at their disposal were keen to display their wealth to the world. The Victorian interior was crammed with objects, and lavish curtains and drapes hung everywhere. The bed was the only place that saw a decline in the use of textiles as bed curtains came to be regarded as unhygienic.

Couple seated on a four-poster bed, c.1475–1503
Israhel van Meckenem (c.1445-1503)

Four-poster bed decorated with
velvets, c. 1700

The 20th century was a period of many different movements and styles. New science and technical progress played a key role. Modernism – a restrained, sober style – continues to have significant influence on the way we design our interiors. But that is only half the story. The 20th and early 21st centuries are characterised above all by the sheer variety and choice on offer. Techniques, yarns and fabrics are being improved all the time, and traditional styles and methods are being rediscovered and newly interpreted. Anything goes, and the range of options is overwhelming. Textile houses – many of them with a very rich history – offer the most beautiful fabrics in countless different styles and colours. We carefully consider what appeals most to our own personal taste, be that old, new, classic or modern, and make our decision. But that is not always easy.

TYPES OF WINDOW TREATMENTS

WINDOW CURTAINS are usually made from opaque material and block out some or all of the light. They are often combined with net curtains or another kind of window covering.

DRESS CURTAINS are curtains that hang at the sides of the window and are not intended to be drawn across.

NET CURTAINS or **VOILE** are the finest of all types of curtain. They filter out the light and soften a room's atmosphere. Net curtains, also known as lace curtains or sheers, often have a lead-weighted hem. Voile is a modern take on net curtains. Some voile fabrics are interwoven with metallic thread.

WINDOW SHADES or **BLINDS** are available in all shapes and sizes – with or without structure, lined or unlined. Blinds without slats tend to exude an air of nonchalance (consider Austrian blinds, for instance) while those with slats (such as Roman blinds) create a neater look.

CURTAIN FABRICS

COTTON is the most widely used natural raw material for textile production. It is strong and versatile, and relatively cheap. The disadvantage of cotton curtains is that, depending on the quality of the cloth, they can fade, crease and shrink.

CHINTZ is a luxurious, usually printed type of cotton, sometimes incorporating a thin coating of resin, but always calendered to give it a characteristic lustre. Chintz is to some extent water repellent and dirt repellent, though it should not be washed – dry clean only. Chintz fabrics are hard to come by in the UK now as they are no longer particularly in fashion

LINEN is produced from the fibres of the flax plant and is one of the strongest and oldest natural fibres. Linen is very popular because of its natural look but, like cotton, it can crease easily and fades when exposed to sunlight. However, in many people's view, that is what gives linen its inimitable look. It is wise to have linen curtains lined as it prevents the fabric from fading and make the creases less obvious. If you prefer to avoid creases altogether, it might be better to opt for a cotton fabric with a linen texture, as there is no such thing as crease-free linen. If the fabric is promoted as being crease free, it is likely to be linen blended with a synthetic yarn. Linen blends particularly well with other fibres such as silk, viscose or cotton.

SILK TAFFETA and **ORGANZA** are available in many gorgeous colours and have a wonderful sheen. Silk is a strong fabric with good insulating properties. Provided that the curtains are made from high-quality silk fabric and are lined, they can last for years or even centuries. Poor-quality silk is more vulnerable, however, and soon deteriorates, especially if the curtains are unlined.

Taffeta is a shiny, slightly stiff fabric which, thanks to the unique way it is woven, produces ever-changing colours and effects as it catches the light. Silk organza is an ultra-fine, sheer fabric with a sense of luxury, although nowadays organza is also blended with synthetic yarns such as polyester or nylon.

SATIN has a renowned lustre thanks to a special weaving method used in its manufacture. There are various types: satin made from pure silk, satin mixed with synthetic fibres, or cotton satin that is made from cotton. The suppleness of the fabric ensures that satin always drapes beautifully.

VELVET/VELOUR is widely used as a curtain fabric and works in any kind of interior, whether contemporary or classic. The material is soft to the touch and has an understated matt lustre. The fabric's nap results in different depths of colour –the colour is accentuated when the fabric is brushed against the direction of the nap. For curtains made with cotton, Trevira CS or mixed-yarn velvets, the pile direction needs to be facing upwards; vicose or patterned velvets should be pile down. Velvet is available in many different colours and styles, so there is something to suit every situation.

A satin paisley fabric

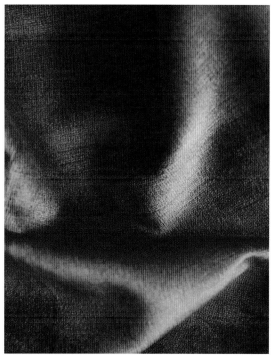

Distressed velvet made from a blend of viscose and cotton

HOW SHOULD I GO ABOUT CHOOSING CURTAINS?

In addition to being functional, curtains also serve as decorative elements in our homes. They offer us the opportunity to play around with luxurious textures, tasteful colour combinations and gorgeous patterns. But how should you apply the latest trends, and where should you start when faced with the overwhelming number of options available? There are infinite possibilities, and that can lead to confusion and make it difficult to know what to decide for the best.

It all starts with taking the time to look and think – the most valuable tips we can give you are: to have faith in your own taste, and dare to be different. In addition to having their own tastes, everyone also has their own opinions, which is why it's better to pay as little heed as possible to other people's thoughts and comments.

– Take your time, have a good look around you and let all the information slowly sink in. Try to see things from a creative perspective, and don't make any rash purchases. Choose something a bit different from a plain and simple curtain fabric – so many other things are possible. Draw inspiration from the information you pick up as well as from photos on the textile houses' websites or in interiors magazines. Take account of the fact that we all have different moods, and that these impact our decision-making. When we're happy, we make different choices to when we're feeling sad. The weather and even the light can influence mood too: we will feel differently about colours and textures in dreary weather than on a bright, sunny day.

– Trust your own judgement because you're more of an expert than you think. Feel free to use interior design trends as inspiration, but it's important to be primarily led by your own feelings and tastes. What's important to you, and what makes you happy? Take a look at your clothes – what are your favourite colours? You wear them, so why shouldn't you use them in your home too? What's your ideal living style – classic, contemporary, eclectic, country cottage or urban?

A comfortable home is one that has a personal feel, one that says something about you – about your soul. A successful interior is one that is a good fit with the architectural style of the property as well as its inhabitants. Try to use fabrics to create an interior that truly reflects you and your lifestyle. Interior design and living magazines can help you to gain a clearer picture of what you like, which styles appeal to you and make you feel at home. You might also find inspiration in works of art, the colours in a photograph, a piece of furniture, a shop window, or a friend's house. Most of all let your own taste lead the way. It's easy to daydream when looking at photos of fantastic interiors, but don't forget that ultimately you're the one who has to live in it. Ask yourself, does it suit you? Is it really you?

– A fresh take on things can work wonders. Try to see the things around you differently, through new eyes. Take a good look at your windowsas this can help you to choose the right material. Think of the window as a painting. The window, including the view through it, is the picture and the curtains are the frame. A pretty view will attract attention to the scenery beyond, so you will need to adapt your fabric choice accordingly. What should you focus on? If it looks out on to a wonderful woodland garden, you could accentuate this and bring the nature from outdoors inside by opting for a pretty floral pattern or oversized roses – it's up to you whether you prefer a modern or more classic style. Curtains with a more subtle motif will lead the gaze towards the garden and create a greater sense of calm, but that is far from the only option. If the view from the window is less appealing, try to focus attention on the interior by using checks or stripes, for example. You can use voile or net curtains to hide a blank wall, a busy street with lots of traffic or an ugly building, thus keeping the undesirable view out of sight. Use your imagination. It is important to hang curtains that you will enjoy looking at day after day, so don't be afraid of patterns – they can help to add balance to a room. Above all, have the courage to just go for it.

– Take the architectural style of the house into consideration. Lavishly draped curtains will look out of place in a minimalist, modern interior, while a plain, simple curtain fabric is a missed opportunity in a classically styled property.

What kind of ambience or image do you want to create in the room? Colour and texture not only trigger our senses, but also influence behaviour. While you may be less aware of texture than of colour, it plays an equally important role. Fabrics can alter the atmosphere within a room with little effort, they can make a room cool and airy in the summer or cosy and welcoming in the winter. You might associate cool comfort with unlined cotton, basic linen or silk, while mohair, velvet or cashmere exudes warmth and luxury. Other fabrics conjure up words such as 'rugged', 'elegant', 'modern' or 'classic'. In the case of rugged, you might think of linen or cotton, whereas silk or damask are considered to be more elegant. Modern wool or synthetic fabrics work well in a contemporary interior, while velour, floral motifs or traditional patterns are associated with a more classical style. But you could also take a completely different approach: rules are made to be broken, and there is infinite scope for experimentation.

Plain curtains can be given a classic touch by adding a trimming of floral fabric or a contrasting colour. A white curtain with a black edging looks dramatically different compared to a plain white one. Use your imagination and think outside the box!

– The type of fabric, pattern, texture and colour you choose are not the only elements that determine the style of your curtains. The size and thickness of the pleats or drapes, the finishing touches of trim or tiebacks, and even the way in which the curtains are hung are all just as important.

– There are many different ways of achieving the ambience to suit you, and the use of layers is one of them. A combination of voile and window curtains in a warm hue creates a tasteful and intimate atmosphere in a room. And don't forget, the more fabric you use, the greater the sense of luxury.

LININGS

Good curtains should always be lined, for the following reasons:
– Lining protects curtain fabrics against sunlight, which causes all fabrics to fade eventually. Generally speaking, light-coloured fabrics fade less quickly than dark ones, but maybe that's because the fading is less apparent. Although dyeing techniques have improved considerably in recent years, turquoise, dark blue, red and black fade the most rapidly. Black curtains should not be hung in direct sunlight unless they are well lined.

– Lined curtains provide insulation. They not only help to deaden sound, but also keep the warmth in and hence save energy. And that's no unnecessary luxury when you consider how much heat can be lost through its windows – sometimes up to 80 percent. Curtains can be hung in front of radiators, but take care they do not hang too close to them, or to window panes for that matter, since condensation, heat and dryness can stain or damage the

fabric and also may cause shrinkage or extension of the curtains. Keep convection heating vents and radiators clean too, since swirls of dust can make curtains (and ceilings) dirty.

– Curtains hang better if they are lined. Interlining with molleton or 'bump' adds extra volume to create a sense of luxury, which is particularly advisable for finer fabrics. A nice lining – perhaps with stripes, checks or another pattern – ensures that the curtains look just as appealing from the outside as they do from inside the room.

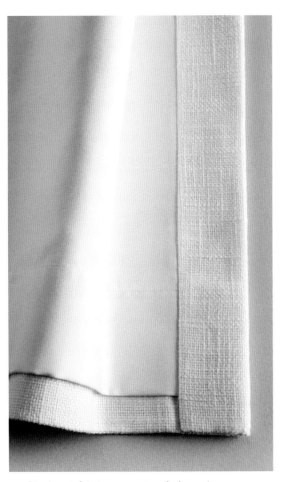

– Line with black-out fabrics if you want guaranteed darkness in a room. Nowadays, it's possible to buy attractive, supple fabrics that can also be used as curtain lining. The bedroom is not the only place for black-out fabric; it can be equally useful in rooms where daylight can be a nuisance, such as nurseries and children's bedrooms, the TV room or home cinemas. If you prefer not to sleep in pitch blackness, it might be better to use dim-out curtain linings. These allow a little more light to penetrate than black-out lining so they do not darken the room completely.

Black-out fabrics guarantee darkness in a room, even when they are white.

A decorative lining means the curtains look as beautiful from the outside as they do from the inside.

Very important: the length of a curtain

When decorating a room, curtains can truly be the icing on the cake.

But keep in mind that curtains that are too short are very unattractive. People often choose to have curtains not touching the ground, to avoid having to clean them too often, because of dust on the hem. But practical is not always beautiful; it is much more appealing to have curtains just touching the floor or even a bit longer.

Curtains covering the radiator can block the warmth, which is why people choose to have short curtains that end on the windowsill. The result is seldom if ever beautiful – blinds are a much better choice.

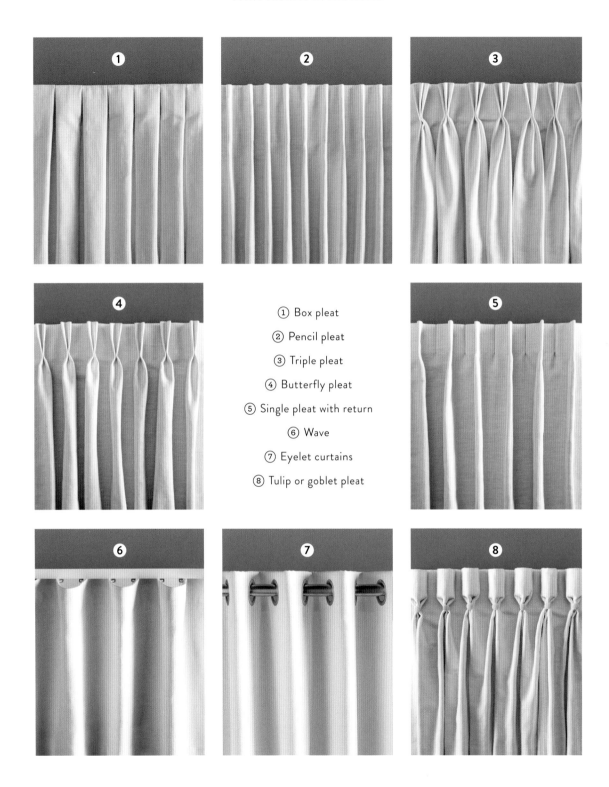

① Box pleat

② Pencil pleat

③ Triple pleat

④ Butterfly pleat

⑤ Single pleat with return

⑥ Wave

⑦ Eyelet curtains

⑧ Tulip or goblet pleat

HEADINGS

The standard width of curtain fabric is around 140 centimetres. The more fabric you use, the better the result. Single-pleated curtains can look a little ordinary; more pleats add fullness and a sense of luxury. There are many different ways of pleating curtains; common types of pleating include the pencil pleat and double or triple pleats such as the butterfly pleat – which is also possible as a single-pleated version. The tulip pleat, or goblet pleat, looks slightly less formal; the pleats are stitched at the bottom and remain open at the top, just like a tulip (or goblet) – they are often padded with foam or kapok to give them a more pronounced shape.

The amount of fabric required depends on the type of pleat you choose, but a good rule of thumb for the best result is to multiply the width of the curtain rail by at least 2.5 times. If your room has a high ceiling, you will need curtains with at least a double pleat to ensure there is sufficient fabric to create gentle folds at the lower edge of the curtains.

What else should I be aware of?

– Get your curtains made and hung by a professional curtain-maker. Curtain-making is a skill, and even the most beautiful fabrics will lose their allure in the wrong hands. A good curtain-maker provides sound advice, can help you to choose the right rails, which is another important aspect, and will allow the fabric to hang for at least six weeks before finally finishing the bottom hems.

– Curtains can extend or shrink. A house 'lives' – heat, humidity and light can affect the dimensional stability of curtain fabrics, causing them not to hang straight. Ideally, curtains should hang for a whole year, through all four seasons, to allow for extension or shrinking before the bottom hem is finally stitched, although for most purposes a few weeks is adequate. Linen curtains are particularly susceptible to lengthening when exposed to heat or humidity, but they also contract again.

– Take the weight of the fabric into account. Curtains measuring 3 metres or more in height can be heavy, so remember this when choosing curtain rails.

– Curtain headings are often made too short. A 5-centimetre curtain heading is much too short and detracts from the overall look of the curtains, which is a shame. Richly pleated curtains with a 12-centimetre heading look much nicer. Remember that the heading should be even taller in high-ceilinged rooms – a heading of 20 centimetres would be ideal in that situation.

– Think carefully about the ideal length of the curtains – they should just touch the floor, or be a little longer. This is particularly important with a tiled or marble floor, since the floor's reflection can cause the curtains to appear too short. That's not a good look, so have the curtains made to be 2 to 5 centimetres longer.

– If curtains have been made slightly longer than necessary and they stretch or shrink because of heat or humidity for instance, there will be enough 'spare' fabric for them to be altered.

– A good curtain-maker will make a seam allowance in the heading. Floor-length curtains will gather dust and dirt, which can increase wear and tear. If you want to lengthen the curtains later – because they have shrunk slightly after dry-cleaning, laundering or changes in atmospheric conditions such as humidity and temperature – and the seam has been stitched at the lower hem, you will be unable to avoid the problem of an ugly edge. You could solve this by finishing the curtains with edging or a trim, but it's a shame if that was not really your intention. By ensuring that the seam allowance is placed in the heading, you will always have enough scope for future alterations.

Shrinkage

Most fabrics will shrink to a greater or lesser extent when washed or dry cleaned. Some will even shrink or extend in use owing to atmospheric variations. What is not commonly known is that shrinkage is not necessarily permanent. Think about it like this: if you cut a square of cotton fabric 30 x 30 centimetres, put it through the recommended wash cycle, dry it and measure it again you will no doubt find that it is no longer 30 centimetres square! So you may wonder where that fabric has gone – it clearly hasn't disappeared! Measure it again, but in the other direction; has it extended? More than likely it has, because what happens when a fabric shrinks in one direction it invariably extends in the other one.

Shrinkage can almost always be regained by judicious ironing. If a curtain has shrunk in the height, iron it while still slightly damp in the direction of shrinkage. You will find that miraculously you will have regained the length you thought you had lost. There may of course be exceptions to this rule: if a fabric has been washed at too high a temperature, or on a too robust cycle in the washing machine, you may have imparted irreversible shrinkage, so you should always follow the care instructions. It is always desirable to err on the cautious side; often the temperature controls on domestic machines are variable and a 30°C setting might be 40°C or more.

The finishing touch

– Pelmets are a good way of concealing curtain rails. In order to ensure the curtains can be drawn smoothly, pelmets should be mounted slightly in front of the curtains rather than directly against them. Pelmets are often made from the same fabric as the curtains themselves, although of course they do not have to be. Just bear in mind that the fabric should not be too heavy.

There are many different types of pelmets – straight, curved or novelty styles – and they may be lined or edged with a pretty trim. The possibilities are endless.

– You could also opt for swags and tails to frame the window and the curtains, but bear in mind that this is specialised work so obtain professional advice beforehand.

– Attractive tiebacks can be used to hold the curtains in place at the side of the window. A wide variety of styles are available in all shapes, sizes and colours, from simple to opulent. Make sure that the curtains are long enough, since tying them back also raises them off the floor, making them appear shorter. If you design your curtains to taper into a point, they will fall perfectly when you tie them back.

– Good curtains require care and attention to ensure they last as long as possible. Vacuum curtains regularly using an upholstery nozzle. Only have them dry cleaned when it is strictly necessary. You can also freshen curtains up by hanging them outside in misty weather.

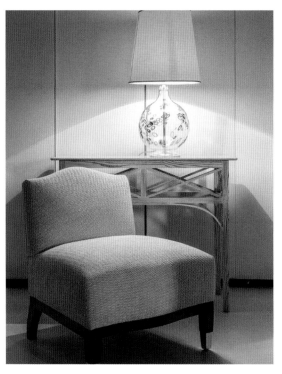

Colour change

Also called metamerism, colour change is a phenomenon whereby printed or dyed colours in a fabric can appear to differ when viewed under different light sources. This can be a significant problem for consumers as the perfect match to their carpet sample when seen in a fabric store can look totally different when they get it home! Fabric manufacturers will carry out their colour matching and control procedures using a light source called Standard Artificial Daylight that replicates, as its name suggests, exterior daylight. Colours matched under this light source can change markedly when viewed under tungsten or fluorescent lighting. Indeed, two different fabrics that appear to be a perfect match in daylight can look wildly different under electric lighting. It is particularly prevalent where a colour is achieved by mixing opposing colours, for example lime green may be achieved by mixing blue and yellow base colours. Also browns and beiges, which are often mixtures of all three primaries – red blue and yellow – can be particularly susceptible.

It is important therefore to always obtain samples of your selected fabrics to study at home under your normal lighting conditions to avoid unfortunate mistakes.

Upholstery fabrics

Upholstery fabrics play a pivotal role in any interior.
The choice of the right fabric for your sofa or chair, in the
first instance is personal taste, but the amount of usage you
envisage in the future should also be considered – in a busy
household with children and pets it is a good idea to choose
upholstery fabric that can withstand the rigours of family life,
rather than a delicate one. However, this certainly does
not mean you cannot make something beautiful of it.

Reconstruction of the bedroom in the villa of Publius Fannius Synistor in Boscoreale,
buried by the eruption of Vesuvius in the year 79CE.

HISTORY

People have always desired warmth and comfort. Of course there have always been those who preach sobriety – the Roman historian Livius (59BCE–17CE) was not in the least bit impressed by the colourful decorations and comfortable cushions with which his contemporaries decorated their homes. Yet we are constantly trying to make our living environments as attractive and comfortable as possible. For centuries, the interiors of the homes of the aristocracy were the most important source of inspiration. Those who could afford to do so, followed these trends, although mostly in a simplified version.

In the Middle Ages, interiors were sparsely furnished. There was very little furniture. Tables were not much more than wooden planks on supports, and people sat on simple benches and stools. Cushions were used only to make sitting down more comfortable. More luxurious folding chairs with seats made of interwoven bands of canvas or leather, and sometimes a back rest of the same material, did exist. The richer the person, the more extravagant the finish – sumptuous fabrics, fat cushions, tassels and fringes made an otherwise simple chair into a status symbol. The expansion of Europe, economic developments, and the growing number of people with money to spend in the 16th century had a huge influence on the development of interior design. Comfort was became increasingly important and thanks to the development of new techniques the first chairs with upholstered seats appeared around 1620. The 'upholsterer' began as a dealer in second-hand goods, but by the end of the 17th century, he had the knowledge and skills to completely upholster chairs and sofas – the comfortable and elegant Louis XV (Quinze) armchair remains very popular to this day.

Up until the discovery of synthetic fibres in the 20th century, wool, linen, silk and later cotton, were the most commonly used fabrics. Silk was a precious material. In the 15th and 16th centuries, silk damasks in particular, were used for (floor) cushions, but by the end of the 17th century, chairs and sofas – and walls – were being covered in the most dazzling array of colours varying from pastel shades to crimson, magenta, deep green, and royal blue. To protect the luxurious upholstery, chairs and sofas often had a loose cover as can be seen in some 18th-century paintings. Linen damask was a cheaper alternative and therefore very popular. In most houses you would find an eclectic mix of chairs covered in all sorts of fabrics and leather that stood against the wall. It was only in the 19th century that people began to experiment with a more nonchalant arrangement – the idea of the comfortable sitting room of today is a 20th-century invention.

For centuries, there has been a definite link between the prevailing trends in interior decoration and fashion in clothes – interior designers are inspired by the fashion designers and vice versa. Trends are a reaction to the times that we live in, the events in society and the needs of the people. Designers try to translate this into interiors as well as fashion. Scottish tartans were originally woven for clothing, for forerunners of today's kilts. But at a certain point people also started to use the cloth for decorating their homes, which in turn inspired new generations of fashion and interior designers, and tartans are still to be seen in many collections today.

Louis XIV armchair upholstered with tapestry
Manufactured by Royale des Gobelins, c. 1755-c. 1765

Madame de Pompadour, 1756
François Boucher (1703–1770)

TYPES OF UPHOLSTERY FABRIC

Pile fabrics

A pile fabric is a textile in which the surface pile (tufts), or nap (fibre ends), is incorporated into the fabric, either standing up or laying on the surface, depending on the material used. The most well known pile fabric is probably velvet, which has been popular for many hundreds of years. Originally, velvet was brought to the Middle East by Kashmiri merchants in the 9th century, and subsequently into Moorish Spain. In Medieval Europe it was developed in Italy in the great silk weaving cities of Lucca, Venice and Genoa. Velvet's soft, luxurious surface appearance and rich dyed shades made it a favourite with royalty and the church for official vestments and it was often further decorated with silk embroidery or woven on gold or silver ground weaves. Its continuing popularity is a testament to its perceived richness and value.

There are many kinds of velvet from the cheapest polyester and cotton right through to the most beautiful silks.

MOHAIR VELVET contains between 70 to 100 percent mohair. It is extremely resilient and durable and is naturally soil resistant. It is available in many colours and designs. It is sensitive to shading and pressure marking, but less so than cotton or viscose velvets.

WOOL VELVET has pile yarns made either entirely or partly out of wool. Just as with mohair, the properties of this material excel in elasticity, colour fastness, and soil resistance. This last attribute is due to the natural oil content of the fibre. Wool velvet is available in many designs and colours. Some qualities of wool velvet are sensitive to shading and crushing.

SYNTHETIC VELVET is a 100 percent synthetic short pile fabric. It is highly resistant to abrasion, easy to care for and available in a wide variety of colours and designs. Synthetic pile fabrics have a polystyrene, acrylic or polyamide content that is often blended with

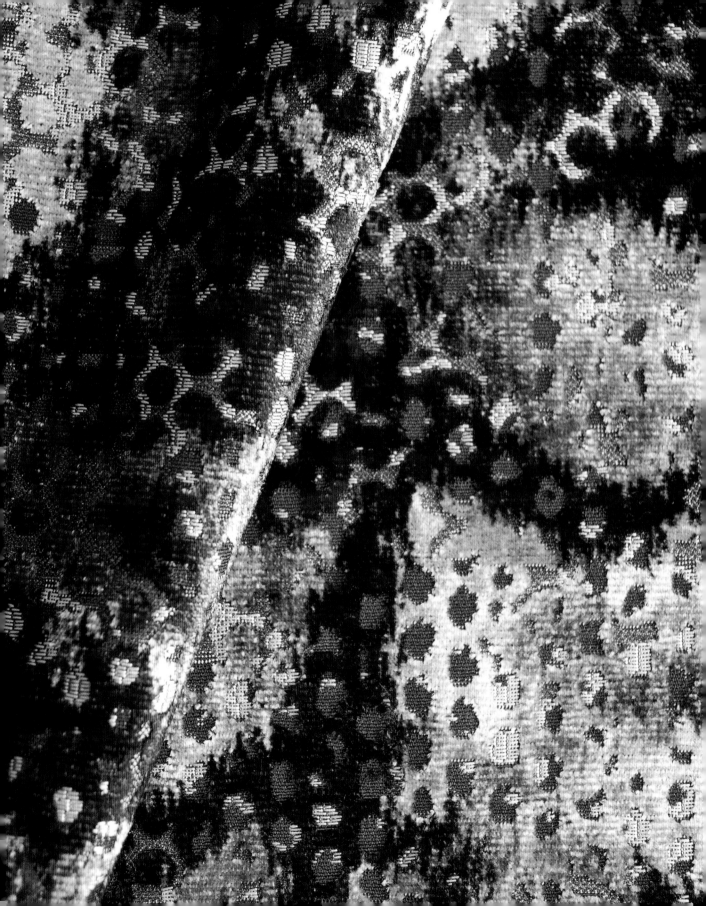

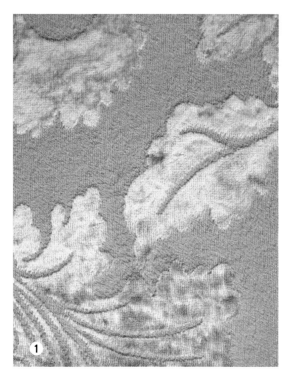

① Velvet made from cotton and viscose ② Flat-weave fabric, digitally printed ③ Epinglé fabric

other fibres. Synthetic velvets are prone to shading and crushing, but the degree is dependent on the quality of the yarn blend. There are also velvets available that are more or less completely crush resistant.

LINEN VELVET has pile yarns spun from flax fibres, which makes for a strong fabric. The linen pile gives the velvet a particular, rather matt appearance and dry feel. This velvet is often woven to give an 'antique' look. It is also expensive compared to cotton or viscose velvet, but is cheaper than silk or mohair.

COTTON VELVET has a dense, close-set pile, which gives it its characteristic soft handle and subtle lustre. Cotton velvets feel lovely and are available in a wide variety of beautiful colours and designs. There are also cotton-synthetic-blend velvets available.

CHENILLE is not strictly speaking not a velvet at all., they have velvet-like apppearance and handle. Chenilles are flat, woven fabrics varying in quality, design and construction. Chenille yarns are often incorporated into patterned or textured weaves to give them a variegated look. They are less prone to shading and crushing than conventional velvets.

DURING USE, THE PILE OF A VELVET CAN BECOME FLATTENED OR DISTORTED, CAUSING DARKER OR LIGHTER AREAS (SHADING AND PRESSURE MARKING). THIS IS QUITE NORMAL AND CAN GIVE A VELVET CHAIR OR SOFA THAT 'LIVED-IN' LOOK.

Flat-weave fabrics

Unlike pile fabrics, and as the name suggests, a flat weave fabric has no surface pile. However it can be variegated in a number of different ways by virtue of its weave technique, yarn selection and method of colouration. The simplest flat weaves are simple plain woven fabrics that are piece dyed to create a solid colour. Alternatively, yarns can be dyed before weaving to create dobby or jacquard patterns of varying complexity. Patterns range from simple stripes through small scale dobby designs to immensely complex brocades and matelassés.

PLAIN WEAVE is usually a plain-coloured fabric that has been piece dyed to create a simple cloth with a multitude of end uses from cushions to curtains, bedcovers and upholstery. Plain-weave fabrics can be cotton, linen, wool, viscose, polyester or mixtures depending on the intended end use. They can be competitively priced, although wools and silks may be at a premium price point.

ÉPINGLÉ is usually woven in wool yarns. Strictly speaking an épinglé fabric, or uncut moquette, is a pile fabric where the loops remainas tight uncut loops on the surface. Occasionally an épinglé weave will have both cut and uncut loops to create a more complex and interesting effect. Wool épinglé has similar properties to wool velvet and is extremely hardwearing. Épinglés may also be woven using different yarn types such as cotton, linen or viscose although those are more unusual.

BOUCLÉ is a fabric that looks very similar to chenille. Bouclé yarns have large and small loops, and are produced using different spinning techniques for the yarns, which creates a surface texture that recovers quickly if flattened, and is more resistant to abrasion.

Quality demands

The colour in furniture fabric should not rub off onto our
clothes, and ideally curtain fabrics would not fade. A number
of internationally recognised quality standards provide a
measure of a textile's colour fastness. It should be borne in
mind that almost all fabrics fade in time, some more than
others. Also, different colours fade to a greater or lesser exent;
generally darker colours can be more colourfast than lighter
shades. The terms used and their meanings are as follows:

Fastness to light The colours may change when exposed to (sun)
light.

Colourfastness during washing With the use of the right
detergents, colours may not fade, run or migrate.

Fastness to rubbing Used especially for upholstery fabrics as it is
important that the colours do not rub off.

Fastness to bleach Few fabrics are able to withstand bleach
and this needs to be taken into consideration when washing
or cleaning fabrics. Most washing powders and detergents
contain bleach or optical brightening agents (OBA).

Fastness to organic solvents When used intensively, the arms of
chairs and sofas can become affected by sweat and natural oils
in the skin.

TAPESTRY WEAVE (NEEDLEPOINT) fabrics are produced using a variety of yarns (cotton, acrylic, polyester, acrylic and viscose). Their durability is largely determined by the density of the weave (thread count per centimetre) and fibre content of the fabric. Usually traditional in design that incorporates 18th and 19th century patterns of flowers, foliage, domestic animals or country scenes.

TWEED was for decades a staple of the British tailoring industry and is now also used, together with its derivatives, for furnishings. The most iconic is of course Harris Tweed, hand woven on the island of Harris in the Scottish Hebrides using pure wool. Wool tweeds, whether Harris or not, can be extremely hardwearing, but require careful finishing if they are not to be scratchy to the touch. Traditionally they incorporate dobby patterns such as houndstooth checks or plaids.

MICROFIBRE or **FAUX SUEDE** is a woven or knitted cloth, in which the surface is 'raised' to create a soft, suede like appearance and handle . The best known of this type of fabric is Alcantara. This and other so-called 'faux suedes' may pill, but there are now varieties that suffer less. By regular brushing faux-suedes will keep looking good. They are usually hard wearing and often have stain resist finishes.

HOW SHOULD I GO ABOUT CHOOSING UPHOLSTERY FABRIC

Just as with curtains there is a huge range of upholstery fabrics. The choice is endless. What sort of sofa are you looking for? Are you looking for a sofa that the whole family can cuddle up on, or do you want a show piece? For many, leather is a safe and practical choice, but you can also have loose covers made for your sofa that can be washed or dry cleaned every so often. There is also no need to go for a simple sofa in a neutral tone, be bold – there are so many possibilities. Think about colour and design: choose stripes, tweed, florals, checks – or a combination – you are bound to be spoilt for choice. Do not be discouraged, there will always be a beautiful fabric to suit your interior and your lifestyle.

– Look around you, think it through; trust in your own style and be daring! Read the section 'How should I go about choosing curtains?' (see page 146) as much of the advice there is just a applicable when choosing an upholstery fabric.

– The price of an upholstery fabric is not indicative of the strength or durability. An expensive fabric is not necessarily strong or wear resistant. Take the time to think about what you want. Will your sofa be a show piece or is it going to be used every day? Do you have a dog or cat that likes to curl up in the corner? Don't forget the effect of their claws either – a beautiful bouclé with tempting loops would not be a good choice.

– Natural oils secreted by the skin – people and animals – are not very good for your upholstery fabric as it destroys the fibres. Medicines in combination with natural skin oils and perspiration can also damage the fabric, in a similar way to small pets walking over the sofa! You can prevent problems like these by having matching loose arm covers and headrests made.

– Loose covers are perfect if you love change. It is a simple way of adapting your sofa or chair according to the season, or you could have a luxurious cover made for special occasions.If you are looking for a fresh crisp look, then you should choose a cotton fabric cover as they can be washed easily, are very hard wearing and last for a relatively long time. You should take shrinkage into account though, but good-quality loose covers are always pre-shrunk.

Choose quality!

Whether you are choosing fabric for a pouffe, curtains, a three-seater sofa or a chair, the final results are largely dependent on the quality you use. The quality of the fabric and fibre blend influences the durability, the degree of crushing or pilling, stain resistance, colour fastness and so on. The use of good-quality fibres – natural, synthetic or a blend – enhances the positive qualities of a fabric. The chair or sofa will not only look wonderful, but will stay looking beautiful for longer, so it is well worth the investment.

What else should I be aware of?

All fabrics have certain characteristics: they can crush (chenille and pile fabrics such as velour or velvet), discolour (cotton, linen, chenille) pill (wool or polyester) or attract dirt.

SHADING AND CRUSHING happens when the pile of a fabric becomes flattened and the surface of the fabric appears patchy. When the pile fibres are not all lying in the same direction, they give the appearance of random marks or look as if water has been spilled on the fabric. This is an optical illusion caused by the nap of a fabric appearing lighter or darker, because of the way it reflects light depending on which way it is lying. The fabric is not actually discoloured and this effect gives the material its charm. Shading may appear quite drastic at first, but some fabrics particularly those with a viscose blend will stabilise in time.

Pile fabrics may be 'crushed' under the influence of body heat, weight and moisture, and shading results. In most cases this can be resolved by brushing with a soft brush. Or you can gently steam the fabric, but allow the treated area to dry for at least six hours before using it again. If needed, contact the manufacture for advice.

PILLING is caused by loose fibres on the surface of the fabric 'felting', or clumping together, as a result of abrasion. It is a common problem, but is a phenomenon that in many fabrics will disappear over time. Ask in the shop or at the manufacturer if the fabric you have chosen is prone to pilling, and whether it is temporary or not. Pilling can be removed using a special fabric 'de-fuzzer' similar to what you might use to 'de-fluff' a jacket or sweater.

WEAR AND TEAR affects all fabrics eventually. The quality of the yarns used and their manufacture, the weave structure and composition, as well as how the fabric is used in the home all determine how long it will last.

The resistance to wear and abrasion of upholstery fabrics is extensively tested. The Martindale test measures the resistance of the threads by rubbing the fabric constantly for hours or even days. How long it takes for the first thread to break will determine a fabric's Martindale figure, but it does not actually give an indication of the strength of the fabric (see page 213). Wear will always occur on the back of a fabric when it is in contact with upholstery padding (foam rubber has an effect a bit like a razor blade).

The sofa or chair itself and what is used inside will determine the life of the covering fabric. The fillings in better, luxury-quality chairs are first covered with a linen or cotton interliner, which not only protects the upper fabric from abrasion but also contribute to a is fuller and more sumptuous furniture.

Accept that at some point you will have to have your sofa re-upholstered. Upholstery fabrics will not last a lifetime and eventually need to be replaced. This means that you can choose a new, entirely different kind of fabric, and just as fashion changes, the chances are that your personal tastes may have changed (a little) over the years too.

A NEWLY UPHOLSTERED SOFA CAN GIVE
YOUR LIVING ROOM A COMPLETELY DIFFERENT,
FRESHER NEW LOOK.

UPKEEP

– Protect furniture from direct sunlight. Modern fabrics generally have good resistance to UV light, but all fabrics will eventually fade. Cotton and linen fabrics tend to be more sensitive to sunlight than wool and synthetic materials.

– Furniture will stay looking beautiful for longer if it is well cared for. Wear and tear is caused by all kinds of things, like pets, sharp objects (such as zips, buckles and jeans studs), and poor maintenance.

– Never break off or pull out snagged threads, but work them through to the back of the fabric with a needle.

– There is no single formula for all upholstery fabrics, but regular cleaning and removing stains correctly will help avoid many potential problems. A weekly vacuum with a soft, smooth brush attachment will help the fabric last longer and keep colours fresh. With pile fabrics, brush with (and not against) the pile. After brushing you can use a damp chamois leather that has been well wrung out to wipe over the arm rests and upper part of the back rests. Fluff can also be easily removed in the same way.

– Turn and plump up the cushions on your chairs and sofas at least once a week and vacuum underneath them.

– Remove stains carefully and correctly. Do not allow spills to dry in, but try and remove as much as possible by dabbing them with kitchen paper, and then carefully cleaning them with warm water or a suitable cleaning solution. For pile fabrics it is not a good idea to try and scratch the marks or stains out as you may also end up pulling out the pile fibres. If necessary, consult the manufacturer's care instructions. It is always best to use a professional on-site cleaning company to remove stubborn stains.

Cushions

Cushions are the perfect accessories for experimenting simply and relatively inexpensively with colour, texture and design. They can make a room more appealing and more comfortable, but to achieve the desired effect, they need to be attractive. They need to have the right dimensions. They need to be well padded and arranged well.

The making of silk, c.1589–93
Philips Galle (1537–1612), after Jan van der Straet

HISTORY

For centuries it was only the elite who could afford hand-woven and embroidered cushions, wall hangings and textiles made of precious and colourful materials. The rest of the population sat on straw-filled cushions made of simple, undyed materials. Around 1400 the majority of textiles produced in western Europe were fabrics made of wool or linen, as they were the only raw materials that were readily available. Spinning and weaving was done at home, and only the aristocracy, the church and wealthy citizens ordered fabric from national and international merchants. In the main, tapestries came from the southern lowlands (Belgium). France and Italy produced silks, damask, and velvet. There was a bustling trade between countries near and far, where raw materials as well as luxury products – for example, stunning woven silk from Constantinople – but also patterns, motifs and even production methods were exchanged.

Kings and princes travelled with an entourage of sometimes hundreds of people, taking furniture from one residence to another. Valuable wall hangings, bed canopies and bedspreads, cushions and blankets were carefully packed and unpacked. The tapissier – the valet who was responsible for the upkeep of all the textiles – had an important job. He was in charge of dressing the chambers with the wall hangings, making up the beds and arranging the cushions and so on. Wall hangings also had an important practical function, they were used as protection from the cold. In the autumn and winter, hangings depicting for example a hunting scene, were hung on the walls, and in spring and summer, they would be exchanged for a more romantic, landscape. Battle scenes and ancient legends were also very popular images. Castles often had a special tapestry room, always hung with beautiful wall hangings and drapes.

Cushions were used to make hard wooden chairs and benches more comfortable and in the Middle Ages, large cushions were often laid on the floor for the women to sit, more or less comfortably. Yet cushions also had a decorative function. In the 16th century, people began to use tapestries in combination with other fabrics, with increasing emphasis on luxury and comfort. Cushions in the 17th and 18th centuries were status symbols often richly decorated down-filled jewels made from tapestry, damask, velvet and embroidery. The 19th century, a time of enormous change, also saw a dramatic change in the comfort of chairs and sofas due to the developments of better springs and thicker padding, but cushions continued to be popular as stylish accessories and were used in great numbers – a trend that has continued right up to the present day.

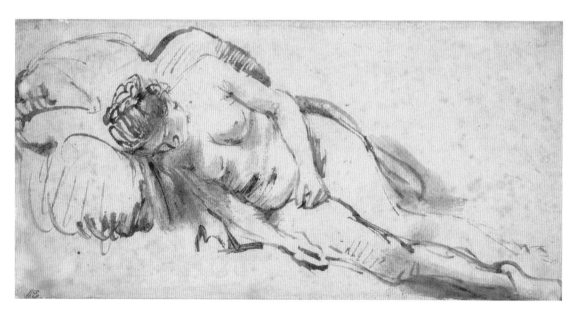

Nude woman resting on a cushion, c.1661-62
Rembrandt van Rijn (1609–1669)

Young girl reading c.1770
Jean-Honoré Fragonard (1732–1806)

HOW SHOULD I GO ABOUT CHOOSING CUSHIONS?

Cushions are versatile accessories that are perfect for styling. Nothing is as inviting as a sofa or chair with beautiful cushions. You can have a fabulous sofa, but without cushions it looks bare – unless of course your preference is for an understated, minimalist interior. Cushions are an easy and relatively inexpensive way to play around with colour, style and texture. You can introduce contrasting accent colours or highlight a colour from the curtains, creating cohesion in your room. Contrasting fabrics or designs can sometimes produce exciting combinations – velvet with tweed, embroidery with checks, leopard-print motifs – the possibilities are endless and will bring your room to life. If your partner likes plain, and you like florals, or if you find your floral print curtains just too much of a good thing, you can still bring in an accent with a pretty floral cushion. So why not choose something different to cushion covers made from the remnants of your old curtain material and play with style and colour – be daring.

What is a good cushion filling?

A beautiful cushion should be plump. It should look inviting and well filled. Well-stuffed cushions – particularly on sofas – are supportive for your back and make the seat more comfortable. A little flat cushion squashed into one of the corners looks awful, and a big, thick wad of stuffing sticking into your back is uncomfortable. So invest in quality. The best cushion pads are stuffed with feathers or down. Down is light and soft, but loses its fullness quickly, whereas feathers give a more stable structure. Check that the cushion pad is not too small. It should be at least 5 centimetres larger than the cushion cover all round.

For those with allergies, kapok-filled cushions are a good alternative. They are slightly firmer and heavier than feather-filled cushions, and they plump up nicely. Kapok-filled cushions are handy for a day-bed or for an outdoor bench, but do not leave them outside as the kapok will go mouldy.

These pictures show how simple it is to change the look of your room without investing in new furnishings.
A fresh set of cushions, a throw, a different side table and some well-chosen accessories is all you need.

Change the style of your rooms with the change of the seasons and use your imagination.
A bit of attention to detail will make all the difference in the world.

BEAUTIFUL CUSHIONS

Regularly plump the cushions up, especially after you have been sitting on them. It not only looks better, but will prolong the life of the filling. There is a trick to fluffing up cushions. Grasp the cushion firmly, hold it with both hands and shake it, this allows air to get back in between the feathers and the down, and the result is a lovely soft, fat cushion. Do not flatten them, as this will break the quills on the feathers.

What else should I be aware of?

A couple of beautiful cushions will bring any sofa or chair to life. It is an easy way to liven up or change a room, and really adds something special. Be careful though as sometimes, too many can make a room look untidy.

TAKE YOUR TIME Think it through, and do not just throw them anywhere. Think about what kind of sofa do you have. Is it plain, patterned, modern or classic? If you have a modern style sofa in a classic interior, you can emphasise the classic by adding a few classic-styled cushions for example. Think of cushions as decoration. Look for beautiful and attractive cushions that compliment your sofa, curtains and interior.

CHOOSING STYLE How you place your cushions is a question of taste, so choose something that you find attractive. Do you like a colourful and nonchalant mix, a stylish combination, or do you prefer clean lines? With plain cushions, be aware of the direction of the weave. It should run horizontally and not vertically, so that the light falls better on the fabric, emphasising the colours and the textures.

CHOOSING SHAPE Look at the different shapes and combinations, or example, use square cushions with oblong ones. Try cushions of different sizes, but bear the proportions in mind. Are they balanced? It is best to work from large down to small. Take a look and see if the format fits with the size of your sofa. There are countless ways of creating different styles.

BE ADVENTUROUS Pay attention to colour and design. The cushions should complement one another, but dare to break the rules! Also consider cushions that have been finished with trimmings – attractive piping, tassels, feathers or beading – again, the options are endless.

BE CREATIVE Don't forget the bedroom either! A few extra scatter cushions and a throw finish off the bed nicely – choose cushions that match the curtains for example, or take inspiration from the colour of the walls or your headboard. Remember to work from large down to small here too.

Washing/Dry cleaning

It is vitally important always to follow the recommended care instructions, normally given in the form of the standard HLCC (Home Laundry Consultation Council) symbols – see table on page 237. Fabric manufacturers provide this information so that their customers can carry out laundering or dry cleaning safely and effectively. It is well known that wash temperature is important, but equally significant is the wash cycle – many fabrics need to be washed with reduced agitation, indicated by a line under the wash symbol.

It is also important to use common sense. Many fabrics are technically washable, but that does not mean that a large pair of lined curtains can be stuffed into a domestic washing machine. Overfilling a machine results in excessive abrasion that can cause colour loss or staining. Equally important is not to start a wash cycle then go off to work or out shopping for several hours before emptying the machine. Although dyes may be colourfast, if they are left in a damp condition in a machine, colour can easily migrate into pale areas of a fabric.

Many fabrics need to be dry cleaned rather than washed or laundered. This is often to avoid excessive shrinkage or to prevent damage to delicate fabrics. Again it is important to follow the care instructions provided by your fabric supplier. The symbol P indicates the use of Perchloroethylene as a dry cleaning solvent, and the line under the symbol is an instruction to the dry cleaner to use a more gentle cycle with reduced agitation. Most dry cleaners are professional and reliable and use high quality solvents, but occasionally there are companies who are less than scrupulous. The British Dry Cleaners Association can provide a list of recommended operators.

For more on this subject see pages 248–53.

How to read fabric labels

– Generally the labels give the name of the collection, the name of the design and a reference number, usually an alphanumeric code that will also indicate the colourway.

– The width indicated on the label is the usable width,or the width between selvedges. The pattern repeat is the vertical repeat (see the section on pattern repeats on page 108)

– The fibre content is a statutory requirement and gives the percentage of each fibre used in the fabric. These can often be abbreviated, for example Co for Cotton, Vi for viscose, Li for linen.

– In the UK and Eire, flammability codes are usually shown. These relate to the fabric's conformity with the UK flammability regulations for fabrics used for upholstery in domestic dwellings.

– Then there are symbols indicating the advised care instructions, using the standardised HLCC symbols, normally including recommendations for wash temperature, use of chlorine bleach, ironing temperature, tumble dry and/or whether spin is advised and finally whether the fabric can be dry-cleaned and if so how.

– There may also be small pictograms to indicate the advised end use.

– Sometimes a 'Martindale' figure is quoted. This relates to a standard test for the durability of an upholstery fabric. Small samples of the fabric to be tested are abraded in a machine and observations are taken at specified intervals until either broken threads are evident or, in the case of pile fabrics, when 'a complete loss of surface pattern or texture' is observed.

– An upholstery grade may also be mentioned; this relates to a scale as laid down in the British Standard BS2543/EN14465 and classifies upholstery fabrics in categories ranging from OD (occasional domestic use), through GD (general domestic use), right up to SC (severe contract use). These classifications are derived from test results for abrasion resistance, tear strength, pilling resistance, colour fastness together with a number of other factors.

Trimmings

Decorative tapes and braids, colourful ribbons, beautiful tassels, fringes and velvety pompoms can be used to create a unique look and are currently rising in popularity again. There is a rich collection of trimmings available that are made from stunning materials for a beautiful, luxurious and highly desirable finish for your curtains, cushions and upholstery.

Portrait of Marten Soolmans, 1634
Rembrandt van Rijn (1606–1669)

HISTORY

Originally, trimmings or *passementerie* were reserved for embellishing clothing. The Egyptians wove gold and silver threads into tape that was then used to decorate their clothes, and the Chinese decorated their robes with tassels. In the Middle Ages, these hand-made treasures spread to palaces, castles, and stately homes. Making them became a specialised job, one that craftsmen spent years mastering before being accepted into the Guild of Passementiers (trimming makers), and they used the most exclusive of materials.

By the 16th century, new techniques meant that the volume and speed of production increased. The use of braids, ribbons, fringes, and tassels grew so fast that in 1531, Charles V, King of Spain, the Netherlands and the Hapsburg empire, decided that only the nobility should be allowed to wear trimmings. In 17th-century France, trimmings were so popular that the trend transferred into interior design – everything was decorated from coaches to furniture. Marie-Antoinette loved them and even had a tassel in her boudoir in the form of a bird cage, complete with bird. Trimmings were not only attractive but also practical as they hid the nails and tacks used to attach upholstery fabric to chairs and settees. Tie backs held heavy curtains open and let the daylight in, and fringes around the bottom of the sofa were useful – when the bottom got dirty, the fringe could be replaced rather than having the whole thing reupholstered.

Pair of gloves made from white leather, trimmed with gold lace and embroidered in
multi-coloured silk, gold thread and sequins, *c. 1622*

However, it was not until the 18th century, the Napoleonic era (Napoleon loved braiding), that trimmings became universally popular. The end of the 19th century was their heyday, when everything from clothing to curtains and lamp shades was decorated.

In the 20th century, things changed and trimmings were perceived as old fashioned and fussy. The trend was towards modern and minimalistic and the production of ribbons, tassels and braids became mechanised. Only a few craftsmen continued to produce hand-made trimmings for a relatively small, but loyal clientele of decorators, interior designers and antique dealers.

There is currently a much greater demand for trimmings and most of the larger fabric design houses present fabulous new collections of tapes, tie-backs and trimmings every year. What is noteworthy, is the modern use of materials such as plastics, metal, leather, rope, beads, feathers, and Swarovski crystal, alongside silky soft yarns and fringes.

Left: *Design for an embroidered edging*, 1765–75
Charles Germain de Saint-Aubin (1721–1786)

HOW SHOULD I GO ABOUT CHOOSING TRIMMINGS?

If cushions are the jewellery to a home's interior, then trimmings are the gem stones. The variety is vast with an array of styles and sizes available – the possibilities are simply endless. Trimmings give an interior that personal touch and make it unique. The best way to choose a trimming is to mix, match and play! You can use trimmings everywhere, on cushions, curtains, sofas, chairs, blinds and throws.

– Choose good-quality trimmings and buy from a reputable maker. Go to the showroom and look through the catalogues. There is plenty of choice, and that applies to price as well as style. You don't have to pay a fortune.

– Look around you. Practically everything can be decorated. Finish blinds off with pompoms, beads or wool. Why should your tie backs be made of a remnant of curtain fabric when you can buy gorgeous chords and tassels? If you choose tiebacks made of fabric, finish them with piping or a trim – or do both! Use the same colour, or beautiful contrasting colours. Piping gives that little extra something to a sofa and makes it look cared for. Instead of piping you could use an attractive chord that will give your sofa a luxurious appearance.

JUST AS YOU CAN SEE IN MANY
HISTORIC HOUSES AND CASTLES, WALL
HANGINGS WERE ALSO FINISHED
WITH TRIMMINGS. BE INSPIRED!

– Finish curtains off with edging – on the sides, at the bottom or all the way round – to protect the fabric from soiling. It looks good, gives a luxurious finish and will help the curtains last longer. Think of velour, a contrasting colour, stripe or check. A broad, dark band at the bottom of a light-coloured curtain looks good, and is also extremely practical as you won't see a dirty hem. You can combine edging with other trimmings too – go simple, elegant, or masculine – it's up to you.

– Lamp shades can also be decorated with trimmings, like Tiffany lights for example. Trimmings will finish a light shade off beautifully. Think about beading, tassels or feathers, or keep it simple with a gorgeous coloured, band of tape or braid – the options are endless here too.

CARE AND
CLEANING

If you want to keep your fabric looking fresh, and help to prolong its life, it's really important to look after it and provide regular maintenance whether it's made into curtains, cushions or covering a chair or sofa. The following tips are important to follow.

GENERAL

– All fabrics will become soiled in use, mainly through the effects of airborne dust and pollution, cigarette smoke and accidental spills or stains. Most of these effects can be avoided or at least minimised.

– Regular use of a vacuum cleaner is essential and can significantly extend the life of furnishing fabrics. Curtains and upholstery should be vacuumed once a week using an upholstery attachment.

– Professional application of a stain-resist treatment such as a Teflon based product can help to prevent soiling, particularly on upholstery.

– Follow the care and cleaning recommendations on the care symbols provided by the fabric supplier.

– Never wait until your fabrics are visibly dirty before washing or cleaning.

WASHING

– Washing is the best way of cleaning small items, depending on their fibre type, and has the advantage that it can be carried out at home.

– Wash fabrics regularly and do not wait until heavy soiling has occurred.

Do not try to wash large items such as full-length curtains or loose covers in a domestic washing machine. The abrasion that results from too large a load can cause fading, shrinkage and creasing.

– Follow the fabric supplier's recommendations regarding temperature, wash method, drying and ironing procedures. These are all indicated by the care symbols (see the key page 237).

– Never use bleaches when washing soft furnishings. Remember too that almost all washing powders contain bleach or optical brightening agents for that 'whiter than white' look. Unfortunately they also have the disadvantage of dulling colours, or causing apparent fading, so use mild liquid detergents for items that will be washed regularly. Nowadays there are specialised detergents and washing powders specifically designed for coloured or dark items.

– Do not soak fabrics for long periods of time, or leave them in a washing machine while still damp, as migration of colour can occur.

DRY CLEANING

– Where dry cleaning is advised make sure the cleaner is made aware of the recommended process. Many types of fabric require careful treatment with reduced agitation, and specific solvents. This is indicated by the care symbols.

– Remember also that there are good and bad dry cleaners – The Association of British Launderers and Cleaners can provide a list of approved establishments.

– It is generally not recommended to use proprietary spot-cleaners or dry-cleaning aerosol sprays, except when they are specifically approved for certain fabric types: It is better to employ professional on-site cleaning contractors.

SHRINKAGE

– All fabrics, particularly those made from natural fibres such as cotton or linen, will shrink to some extent. It is quite normal for furnishing fabrics to shrink during washing, sometimes by as much as 6 to 8 percent.

– Dry-cleaning (which, of course, is not a 'dry' process at all) can also cause shrinkage, although generally to a lesser degree.

– Much of the shrinkage caused in washing can be regained by ironing the fabric while still slightly damp in the direction of shrinkage and gently stretching it as you do so.

– It is generally accepted that wash temperature is an important factor but equally significant are the effects of mechanical agitation and drying temperature and method. Again be careful to follow the instructions given by the care symbols.

– Take care not to dry washed items too quickly. Tumble-drying should be avoided whenever possible, as it can cause creasing and shrinkage. Curtains should always be made with an adequate hem, loosely tacked until after the first washing or cleaning. An allowance of at least 5 percent should be added to the length required.

– Side seams or attached linings should be hand stitched to allow for differential movement between face fabric and lining. Always use a thread of the same fibre as the fabric you are sewing.

– Curtains may shrink or extend in use owing to fluctuations in atmospheric temperature and humidity. This is particularly so with fabrics containing a high proportion of viscose.

– Make sure that curtains do not hang too close to windows or radiators where either excessive moisture from condensation or excessive heat and dryness can have dramatic effects in terms of dimensional stability and soiling.

LIGHT FASTNESS

– Printed or dyed furnishing fabrics nowadays have good inherent resistance to fading in light, but all fabrics do fade eventually.

– Curtains and blinds should always be lined and, if possible, drawn right back from the windows during daylight. Do not assume that because you live in a northern climate your curtains will not be affected – the damaging UV rays in sunlight, which cause fading, do penetrate cloudy skies!

– Shutters or sun awnings will give added protection in sunny areas.

– Sheer curtains and voiles are particularly vulnerable to fading. Whenever possible hang lining curtains to protect them.

– Silk curtains should always be lined to protect them from UV light.

SPECIFIC INSTRUCTIONS
for fabrics and furniture

SILKS

It is well known that silk fabrics can be more fragile than other types and a certain amount of care should be exercised in their make up and maintenance.

- Silk curtains should always be lined to protect them from sunlight, and should not be used for Roman blinds where any degree of fading will be more obvious.
- Silk should always be dry cleaned by professional cleaners with experience of furnishing fabrics, and be cleaned using the careful cycle as indicated in the Care Symbols.

LINENS

Linen fabrics, whether 100 percent linen or mixed with other yarns such as cotton or viscose, are more prone to shrinkage than other fibre types, especially in washing. For this reason it is recommended that all linen fabrics should be dry cleaned. Where linen fabrics are recommended to be suitable for washing, they may have been given a pre-shrunk finish in order to minimise shrinkage. This may result in curtains extending once hung. So, a loosely stitched hem is advisable then that curtains may be adjusted once they have 'settled in'.

VELVETS

A luxurious and beautiful fabric, velvet comes in many different types, from simple plain cotton velvets through to more extravagant multicoloured, jacquard-woven designs. They all need to be handled and treated with care. The surface pile is vulnerable to pressure marking both during make up and in use, but if you follow a few simple rules you can achieve excellent results.

- For curtains you should make up velvet with:
  - pile upwards: for cotton velvets, Trevira CS velvets and velvets made of mixed yarns.
  - pile downwards: for shiny (viscose) velvets and velvets with a pattern.
- Making curtains with the pile facing up gives a deeper and fuller colour but if you make up viscose velvets with the pile upwards you will lose a lot of the lustrous, shiny effect. It is also strongly recommended that velvet curtains are lined to prevent pile loss and fading through sunlight. Lining also gives far better draping and thus a more beautiful general appearance.
- You should always use a pull cord or rod to open and close your velvet curtains; too much hand contact will bruise and crush the texture of the pile, and, eventually, you will be able to see handprints where you grab your curtains to pull them back.
- Make sure that the velvet you choose for upholstery is suitable and apply the right techniques. This means seaming the cut edges and folding the edge twice before nailing or stapling the velvet to prevent the fabric from unnecessary splitting or tearing. Do not make up velvet directly onto foam

fillings, but use an interliner even if the velvet has been backcoated. The fabric will last longer and pile-loss will be reduced.

– Cotton velvet is a natural product. When made up for curtains or on a sofa, it will obtain its unique appearance after some time in use, due to pressure and the natural humidity of the environment. Pressure marks, rolling stripes and smaller irregularities, which are inherent in the product, will disappear in a ventilated and relatively humid environment. Steam or distilled water through a sprayer will enhance this process (not to be used on viscose or flame retardant cotton velvets). To return the pile to its original condition and appearance, steam and brush it with a soft brush.

– Dry cleaning is the preferred method for virtually all velvets although some Trevira CS velvets can be machine washed gently at 30°C. The best way to dry velvets after washing is a natural drying process rather than tumble drying.

FURNITURE

Buying furniture is often the result of long deliberation and careful choosing. If you want to enjoy your purchase for many years, and ensure it has a long life follow these easy rules.

– When furniture has loose seat and back cushions, plump them up daily. Turn them and rotate the position of cushions every month. This will prevent uneven or excessive wear.

– Tight upholstery should be cleaned on site by a professional cleaning specialist.

– Do not spot cleaning with proprietary products yourself; this should only be carried out oy a professional cleaning specialist.

– Where seat or back cushions have removable covers do not be tempted to wash or clean them separately as colour changes will eventually become evident.

– Although most furnishing fabrics have good resistance to fading, we do advise that furniture should be protected from exposure to strong sunlight.

– Velvet upholstery generally can be prone to marking caused by pressure in transit or in use. Most pressure marks can be removed by gently steaming and brushing with a soft brush.

– Shrinkage can be a major factor with loose covers. If they are too loose unsightly, however, it is also a mistake to make them too snug as even with dry cleaning they will be impossible to refit satisfactorily. The best method is to launder the fabric prior to making up the cover in order to eliminate as much of the residual shrinkage as possible. Where this is not feasible, try re-fitting the covers while they are still slightly damp and allow them to dry on the chair or sofa.

– Do not allow animals onto your furniture – they can cause more damage in a short time than years of normal use. Also children's shoes and buckles or studs on jeans can easily pluck threads from the surface of fabrics.

KEY TO CARE SYMBOLS

HAND WASH

DO NOT WASH

MACHINE WASH GENTLE

WASH AT 30°C

WASH AT 30°C CAREFUL CYCLE

WASH AT 40°C

WASH AT 40°C CAREFUL CYCLE

DO NOT BLEACH

DO NOT IRON

COOL IRON TEMPERATURE

MEDIUM IRON TEMPERATURE

HOT IRON TEMPERATURE

DRY CLEAN

DO NOT DRY CLEAN

TUMBLE DRY

DO NOT TUMBLE DRY

TUMBLE DRY COOL TEMPERATURE

TUMBLE DRY MEDIUM TEMPERATURE

PROFESSIONAL DRY CLEAN

GLOSSARY 1
COMMONLY
USED FABRICS

ACETATE A man-made, natural polymer fibre based on cellulose, often referred to simply as Rayon. It is used generally as a filament yarn to produce fabrics resembling silk.

ACRYLIC A man-made, synthetic fibre derived from polyvinyl that can be textured and spun to produce a yarn similar to wool in handle and appearance. Various modified qualities exist mainly to confer extra advantages such as flame retardancy.

BROCADE A figured fabric, jacquard woven and generally multicoloured in which the pattern is produced by floating the warp and/or weft yarns. Traditionally brocades were woven in silk, but nowadays many other yarns are used such as cotton, viscose and acetate.

BROCATELLE A heavy furnishing fabric in which the pattern is brought into relief by the warp threads raised over a closely woven background weave.

CALICO A generic term for a lightweight, plain-weave cotton fabric. Calico is heavier than muslin.

CANVAS A generic term for heavy fabrics usually made from cotton, linen or jute in a plain-weave construction. The main feature of these fabrics is their close-set weave structure.

CASHMERE Fibres from the downy underbelly of the Asiatic Kashmir goat. They are woven to produce an extremely soft and luxurious fabric.

CHENILLE A pile fabric woven using chenille yarns, usually in the weft, to produce a fabric usually softer and less uniform in appearance than velvet. The yarn is produced by binding short fibres (2-3mm) into twisted yarns to form the distinctive velvety appearance and handle.

CHINTZ A glazed, usually printed, plain-weave fabric of cotton where the chintz finish is produced by calendering. The term fully glazed or resin-glazed denotes fabrics that have been impregnated with resin or starch to give a more durable finish. It should be noted that no cotton chintz finish is permanent and will be progressively reduced in dry cleaning and completely removed if the fabric washed by hand or in a machine. *See also* Calender, Glossary 2

COTTON The most common textile fibre in use today, cotton derives from the seed hair of a wide variety of plants in the *Gossypium* family. It has been in continuous use as a textile fibre for at least 5,000 years. Nowadays cotton is grown all over the world and its characteristics and properties vary enormously according to country of origin and type. Fibre length varies from less than 2.5 centimetres for short-staple types to 10 centimetres or more for long staple ones. Generally speaking the longer the staple length the finer the quality of cloth that can be woven from it. *See also* Fibres, Egyptian cotton *and* Glossary 2.

CUPRO A man-made fibre, similar to viscose, made from cotton linter, the downy fibre around the seeds.

DAMASK A fabric usually of jacquard construction and usually self-coloured in which the pattern is produced by the contrasting lustre or reflection created by warp and weft satin weaves. *See also* Jacquard.

DUCK A closely woven, plain-weave cotton cloth similar to canvas in construction, but lighter. Duck is mainly used as a base for printed fabrics.

DUPION A rough, slubby silk yarn. Nowadays the term usually describes a fabric made from silk or rayon that has a deliberately pronounced slub effect in the weft.

ECRU A French term for greycloth that has passed into common English usage to denote an unbleached, undyed fabric in a natural colour. *See also* Greycloth

EGYPTIAN COTTON An exceptionally fine cotton fabric made with long-staple cotton fibres – the finest in commercial cultivation. This fibre spins a much finer and smoother yarn, making it ideal for bedlinen. *See also* Sea Island cotton *and* Fibre, Spinning, Glossary 2

GINGHAM A plain-weave, lightweight fabric made with dyed yarns to produce the typical small check design, usually a single colour with white.

GREYCLOTH/GRIEGE Fabric as it comes off the loom prior to subsequent bleaching, dyeing or printing. Also described as loomstate. *See also* Ecru

HOPSACK A heavy fabric with a modified plain weave formed by weaving two warp and/or two weft yarns as one, which gives it its a characteristic hopsack effect.

IKAT A fabric produced by the Ikat method that originated in Indonesia and Malaysia where the design is produced by selective resist dyeing of the warp and/or weft yarns prior to weaving to create the typical soft geometric design.

INTERLINING A thick, soft fabric used between the curtain fabric and the lining material. It has a raised and/or brushed surface finish and provides good sound and heat insulation and keeps out the light.

JACQUARD A type of loom mechanism that permits the control of individual warp yarns in an unlimited repeat size by means of punched cards or electronics. - Fabrics woven on jacquard looms usually have large designs that may be piece dyed as in the case of damasks or yarn dyed, for example with tapestries, brocades and lampas.

JASPÉ A fabric having a vertical shaded appearance that is created by using different shades of colour in the warp in a fine stripe arrangement.

LAMPAS A multi-coloured figured fabric similar to brocade, usually made of silk, cotton or a combination of yarns.

LINEN Yarns spun from, or fabric woven from flax fibre. *See also* Flax

LINING A fabric used for lining curtains, blinds and bedcovers to give some protection from fading or to improve the drape or other characteristics.

LOOMSTATE *See* Greycloth

MODACRYLIC A modified (usually "FR modified") acrylic fibre, or yarn spun from this fibre.

MOIRÉ Traditionally moiré describes an effect created by passing fabric under tension across specially configured combs; this is not long-lasting. Permanent moiré can be created by subjecting fabric to heat and heavy pressure on specially constructed rollers, to create a 'rippled', or watermarked, appearance. The effect is results from the way the flattened and unflattened parts of the fabric reflect light. The term moiré is also incorrectly used to describe fabrics where the watermark effect is produced by printing the moiré pattern on to the surface of the fabric or weaving it as a jacquard design.

MOQUETTE A patterned upholstery fabric with areas of warp pile where the loops are left intact (uncut moquette), or where the loops have been cut by wires or blades (cut moquette). Cut moquettes can also be produced by face-to-face weaving. *See also* Velvet

MUSLIN A lightweight open-, plain- or simple-weave fabric.

OTTOMAN A fabric with a pronounced horizontal rib effect produced by weaving a fine, close-set warp over thick and/or bunched weft yarns. Originally made with a silk warp and wool weft but nowadays more usually a cotton, mercerised cotton or viscose warp and a cotton weft. Ottoman may be plain coloured, striped or interwoven with dobby or jacquard designs.

PERCALE A fine, closely woven plain-weave fabric, usually of Egyptian cotton and lighter than Chintz. May be plain or printed, glazed or unglazed.

PIQUÉ A fabric of double-cloth construction with a distinct padded or wadded appearance created by weaving a fine plain weave construction over heavy weft yarns. Piqué fabrics often have a quilted appearance. *See also* Matelassé, Glossary 2.

PLAIN WEAVE The simplest of all the weave constructions in which the warp yarns interlace alternately over and under the weft yarns. This results in a very even, flat construction when yarns of equal size are used in warp and weft. Quite pronounced ribbed or slubbed effects are produced when the yarns are of markedly different size or type.

POLYAMIDE A type of nylon used either as fibres, spun into yarn, often blended with cotton, or as continuous filament yarn. *See also* Fibre, Filament yarn, Glosssary 2

POLYESTER A man-made synthetic-polymer fibre resembling cotton. Widely used for clothing and bed linens owing to its excellent abrasion resistance and easy care properties.

POPLIN A lightweight, plain-weave, cotton-type fabric with close-set warp yarns that produce a fine horizontal rib.

RAYON A generic term for a number of regenerated cellulose fibres and the yarns produced from them. Examples are: viscose, acetate, Modal and Cupro. *See also* Viscose

SATIN/SATEEN These terms have become more or less synonymous with one another as both are smooth fabrics produced by 'floating' yarns, conventionally over four threads (known as 4-and-1). A *Satin* is a fabric where warp yarns float over weft, and *Sateen* is where weft yarns float over warp.

SEA ISLAND COTTON Another exceptionally fine, long-staple type of cotton originally grown on Sea Island, off the coast of Georgia, USA. Varieties include American Pima and Eygptian cotton. It is grown in very small quantities as it is more difficult to cultivate than other types. *See also* Egyptian cotton *and* Fibre, Spinning, Glosssary 2

SHEER A generic term for various kinds of semi-transparent fabrics such as voile, muslin, organdie and net. *See also* Muslin, Voile

SILK The fibre, yarn or fabric produced from the natural protein secretion of the (generally cultivated) silk moth larva that is unreeled as a continuous filament from the cocoons. *See also* Fibre, Filament Yarn, Glosssary 2

TAFFETA A plain-weave, closely woven, smooth and crisp fabric with a faint weft-way rib and typically 'crunchy' handle. Traditionally of silk, but nowadays can be silk/viscose and other silk mixtures.

TAPESTRY Originally a closely woven fabric in which coloured threads were inserted by hand to produce a figured pattern. Nowadays the term is more loosely used to describe figured fabrics in which the pattern is created by the use of coloured yarns in the warp and/or weft on a jacquard loom, often using two or more different types of yarn in each direction.

TOILE French word for fabric and now also implies fabric of a certain type for example, a plain-weave, light- to medium-weight cotton

TUSSAH SILK A coarse, uneven silk produced by the cocoon of the wild silkworm. It is generally beige or brown in appearance and is usually a spun yarn as the filament cannot be reeled in the same way as cultivated silk.

TWILL A fabric with a diagonal rib effect produced by a weave construction not unlike that of a drill or satin.

VELOUR A pile fabric with the pile (or tufts) laid in a single direction creating a smooth appearance.

VELVET A pile fabric in which the pile (or tufts) are woven into the warp. The effect is produced in one of two ways: either by the weaving of loops that are cut as wires are withdrawn from each row, or by effectively weaving two fabrics face to face, joined together by the pile thread, which are then separated by a knife as the fabric comes off the loom.

VISCOSE A manufactured (regenerated) fibre produced by the viscose process from a cellulose base – mostly from specially cultivated coniferous trees or cotton linter. It resembles cotton in its chemical make-up and quality and may be continuous filament or spun yarn. In furnishing fabrics it is invariably blended yarn with cotton or used as a mixed fabric with cotton or linen. It generally has a more lustrous appearance than cotton, particularly when used for the pile in a velvet.

VOILE A very lightweight, open-weave fabric that is made from fine yarns, typical of 'net' curtains. *See also* Sheer

WOOL Yarns spun from, or fabric woven from animal fibres. Most is made from sheep or lamb's wool, but it can be Angora rabbit, goat (Angora or Kashmir) or Alpaca. *See also* Fibre, Glossary 2

GLOSSARY 2
COMMONLY
USED TERMS

ABRASION RESISTANCE The ability of a fabric to resist the effects of abrasion in use. This is measured using the Martindale Abrasion Test and is a measure of the relative wearability of fabrics in upholstery use. Small samples of the fabric to be tested are mechanically rubbed against a standard abradant material and the number of cycles (rubs) is assessed at 'end point' i.e. when a number of threads are broken or, in the case of velvets or other pile fabrics, until complete loss of surface texture. *See also* Martindale

ARMURE French word meaning weave effect.

BLEACH, BLEACHING A process for improving the whiteness of textiles by removing natural colouring matter from the cloth. *See also* OBA

BLEND To mix fibres of different types together to form a yarn with improved characteristics. For example nylon may be blended with cotton or wool to give increased strength and abrasion resistance, viscose may be blended with cotton to give increased lustre. Generally the fibres are blended during the spinning process to ensure consistency of end product.

BOW A visible fault in printed or woven fabrics caused by a curvature or distortion in the warp or weft during processing. It is difficult to completely avoid this effect, especially with fabrics that are subject to wet processing, such as printed or plain-dyed fabrics.

BUMP *See* Interlining, Glossary 1

CALENDER A machine in which heavy rollers rotate under pressure, like a mangle. The rollers are usually heated and one of them is highly polished and imparts a glazed finish to fabric (*see* Chintz). The fabric is often impregnated first with resin in order that the resultant glaze effect is more durable.

CARDING/CARDED The untangling, cleaning and removal of foreign matter from textile fibres to produce a continuous web of fibre suitable for subsequent processing into yarn. The process is carried out by passing the raw material through revolving rollers that are covered with pins or 'cards' that resemble those in a musical box.

CARE LABELLING An internationally recognised scheme for the labelling of all textiles using standardised symbols to indicate the appropriate washing, cleaning, ironing methods for a given fabric or item of clothing.

COLOUR FASTNESS The ability of a fabric or wallpaper to resist the fading caused by sunlight, washing, dry cleaning etc. The internationally recognised system in use is the British Standard BS1006 in which colours are tested and rated on a scale from 1 to 8, in which 8 is the most colourfast and 1 the least. A standard of 5 for upholstery fabrics and 5/6 for curtain fabrics is considered to be an acceptable level. The scale for washing, dry cleaning and rubbing is 1 to 5. *See also* Fade, Fading

COLOUR WOVEN A fabric in which the pattern is created by dyeing the yarns prior to weaving. *See also* Dyes, Piece dyed

COMBED YARN Fine-quality cotton yarn in which the fibres have been combed rather than carded prior to spinning. This gives a smoother, finer and more lustrous yarn. It is normally only used for the best quality, long staple cottons such as Egyptian or Sea Island. *See also* Carding *and* Egyptian Cotton, Sea Island cotton, Glossary 1

CONSTRUCTION A method of describing the way a fabric is constructed. It commonly states the fibre type, the number of warp and weft yarns per inch or centimetre, and the count and type of those yarns. *See also* Count, Fibre, Warp, Weft, Yarn

COUNT Also known as yarn count, this is a method of expressing the relative thickness of a textile yarn, either in terms of weight per unit length or as length per unit weight. For example, English cotton count is the number of 840 yard lengths to the pound; Denier is the number of grammes per 9,000 metres.

CROSS DYED Fabric woven from different yarns, – for example, cotton and polyester, cotton and modacrylic –in which one of the components takes the dye differently to the other, resulting in a two-tone effect.

DIMENSIONAL STABILITY The ability of a fabric to resist the effects of shrinking or elongation during use or in washing or dry cleaning. There is a British Standard test to measure this and the result is quoted in percentage terms, for example, 3 per cent shrinkage indicates that the fabric will shrink 3 centimetres in every metre. Dimensional Stability can vary considerably from one type of fabric to another. *See also* Shrinkage, Sanforised, Pre-shrunk.

DIRECT DYE *See* Dyes

DOBBY Originally, and still, a mechanism for controlling a loom to create a pattern in the weave. More usually now the term describes the style of fabric woven on such a loom, usually a small-scale repeating design either colour-woven or piece-dyed.

DRAPE The term used to describe the ability of a fabric to hang in graceful folds, which makes it suitable for curtains. There is a British Standard test to measure the degree of drape in a fabric.

DRILL A heavy twill fabric of similar construction to a denim, but often also with a satin face.

DRY CLEAN To clean a textile article by treatment with an organic solvent as distinct from a water based solution. Examples of such solvents are white spirit, perchloroethylene and trichloroethylene, although in the UK today the only authorized solvent is perchloroethylene.

DURABLE FINISH Any type of finish reasonably resistant to normal usage, washing and/or dry cleaning, in particular relating to flame retardant finishes.

DYES A colourant, usually organic, which is designed to be absorbed by or made to react with a fabric in order to impart colour with some degree of permanence. There are several types:

- *VAT DYES* impart a high degree of colour fastness to light, washing and dry cleaning. Their fastness results from their chemical make-up in that the dye is applied to the cloth in a modified form and is subsequently processed so that the dye solution bonds to the fabric at a molecular level and is almost impossible to remove.

- *REACTIVE DYES* also bond to the cloth, but not as permanently as Vat dyes. Their main advantage is that it is possible to achieve extremely bright and vivid colours that are reasonably fast to washing, but not particularly fast to light. For this reason they are used mainly for clothing.

- *DIRECT DYES* are simple to apply to cloth and have good fastness to light, but rather poor fastness to washing. They are therefore quite suitable for heavier fabrics that require dry-cleaning.

Traditionally, British printers and dyers have used vat dyes and still continue to do so. Nearly all the fabrics produced in the UK, and most of those produced overseas, use vat dyes. Many European manufacturers rely on direct or reactive dyes. *See also* Colour fastness, Fading, Piece dyed *and* Colour woven.

END A term used to describe the warp yarns in a woven fabrics. Weft yarns referred to as picks.

END USE Advice as to the suitability of fabrics for a given purpose, in terms of their level of wear for example, suitable for contract or domestic use anas well as an indication of their suitability for curtains, loose covers, upholstery or bedcovers. The suitability is determined by consideration of a number of factors such as abrasion resistance, tear strength, drape and colour fastness.

ÉPINGLÉ *See* Moquette, Glossary 1

FADE Also decribed as fading, this is a change in the colour of a fabric caused by one of a number of different factors such as light, washing, dry cleaning and abrasion. The change is normally one of a reduction in depth of shade, but can equally be one of colour change due to the loss of one or more of the component colours in the dye formula.

FASTNESS *See* Colour Fastness

FAULT An unwanted defect in a fabric caused by one or more of the many different weaving, dyeing or printing problems that can occur, such as knots, neps or slubs in weaving, out-of-register or bowed printing, or uneven dyeing.

FIBRE The basic textile raw material that occurs in many different forms and is spun into yarns to produce fabrics. The broad categories of fibre are:

- *NATURAL FIBRES* occur in nature and are from animal (protein based), vegetable (cellulose based) or, more rarely, mineral origins. Wool, silk, cotton and linen are all examples of natural fibres.
- *REGENERATED FIBRES* are formed from a solution of naturally occurring polymers and having the same chemical constitution as the substance from which they are derived. The most common types in furnishing use are based on cellulose polymers for example, viscose, acetate and Cupro.
- *SYNTHETIC/MAN-MADE FIBRES* are produced from polymers built up from chemical elements or compounds in contrast to those made from naturally occurring fibrous substances. Acrylic/Modacrylic, polyester and Nylon are the most common man-made furnishing fibres.

FIGURED FABRIC A fabric in which the pattern is produced by a combination of different weave structures and yarn colours created either by dobby or jacquard looms.

FILAMENT YARN A yarn made from a continuous fibre or fibres as distinct from a yarn spun from staple fibres. The only naturally occurring filament fibre is silk. All synthetic man-made fibres are manufactured as continuous filaments and may be used as they are or chopped into staple fibres and spun into yarn.

FINISH A term broadly used in the textile industries to denote:

- A chemical substance added to a fabric during processing in order to impart various desired properties such flame retardant, easy care, shrink resistance and/or soil/stain resistance.
- A mechanical process carried out on a fabric to produce a desired effect for example, compressive shrinkage, calendering, or glazing

FLAME RETARDANT Also known as fire retardent, this is a substance or treatment (for example, Pyrovatex, Proban, Back-coating) that is applied to a fabric to suppress, or significantly reduce, the propagation of flame. Also a term to describe fabrics so treated or those made from inherently flame-retardant yarns such as Trevira CS or Modacrylic.

FLAX The fibre extracted from plants of the species *Linum usitatissimum* that is processed to produce linen fabrics.

FLOAT A length of yarn that 'floats' over a number of other yarns in a woven fabric. This is typical of satins, damasks and other jacquard-woven fabrics.

FOLDED YARN Also described as twisted or doubled, this is yarn in which two or more single yarns are twisted together to form a new one that is stronger, finer, more lustrous and more abrasion resistant than a single one of the same combined size and weight.

GLAZE A smooth, glossy finish on a fabric deliberately produced by calendering, usually in conjunction with resin impregnation. *See also* Calender *and* Chintz, Glossary 1

GREYCLOTH/GREIGE *See* Glossary 1

HANDLE The quality of a fabric as judged by the sense of touch in terms of such characteristics as roughness/smoothness, harshness/suppleness and warmth/coolness.

IGNITION SOURCE An applied source of heat such as a cigarette, match or crib 5, that is used to atttempt to ignite fabric in flammability tests.

LINEN UNION Originally a fabric woven with a linen warp and cotton weft, to give a characteristic 'slubby' appearance. Nowadays it is more usually woven with a cotton warp and linen weft

MARTINDALE A machine used for measuring the resistance of a fabric to abrasion (rubs), as a means to assessing wearability in upholstery use. Small samples of fabric are mechanically rubbed against a standard abradant material and the number of cycles (rubs) is assessed at 'end point' – when a number of threads are broken. *See also* Abrasion resistance.

MATELASSÉ A double or compound fabric with a quilted appearance sometimes accentuated by the use of wadding threads.

MERCERISATION The treatment of cellulose yarn or fabric (usually cotton) with a caustic solution to enhance various qualities such as lustre (sheen), the ability to take colouration, strength and stability. It is used particularly for satins and damasks to enhance lustre and drape. It is named after the British chemist John Mercer (1791–1866) who discovered it in 1844.

METAMERISM The phenomenon whereby the colour of an object appears to change in different lighting. Typically it may be noted that two fabrics seem to be an identical match under daylight, but under domestic lighting (tungsten) or "office" lighting (fluorescent) they are no longer the same and appear to be very different shades to each other.

MIXTURE/MIXED YARN A yarn or fabric composed of fibres of different types spun together to give improved characteristics to a fabric. For example, the use of nylon in cotton warps to give increased strength and abrasion resistance. *See also* Blend

NAP The surface effect of a fabric produced by raising and/or brushing to create an appearance and handle similar to the pile of a velvet but much shorter.

NATURAL (FABRIC) Fabric that is undyed and has no finish or colour. *See also* Ecru, Greycloth, Glossary 1

NEP A small knot of entangled fibres that form a raised knot-like fault in cloth; a short slub. *See also* Slub

OMBRÉ A French term meaning shaded that is used to describe a fabric in which the colours are graduated from light to dark in stripes of varying shades. *See also* Jaspé, Glossary 1

OBA (Optical Brightening Agent) Sometimes called FBA (Fluorescent Brightening Agent) this is a substance used to increase the apparent whiteness or brightness of fabrics by converting ultra-violet radiation into visible light. It can be applied to fabrics during processing and is also found in most proprietary washing powders and detergents.

PAISLEY A decorative design based originally on an Indian pinecone motif that has been popular since the 17th century. It has subsequently been produced in thousands of variations, both printed and woven and was particularly used for shawls. The name originated from the town of Paisley near Glasgow where this style of design was woven in the 18th century using the early imported designs.

PATTERN REPEAT The size of one complete unit of a design in both vertical and horizontal directions. For practical purposes normally only the vertical dimension is quoted as it affects calculations of quantity of fabric required for curtains, for example. Repeats may be straight- or half-drop, and this must be taken into account when buying fabric.

PICK The term used to describe the weft yarns in woven fabric. *See also* Ends

PIECE DYED Plain-coloured fabric that is dyed 'in the piece' after weaving (as opposed to the yarns being dyed beforehand). *See also* Colour woven, Dyes

PILE Surface effect on a fabric formed by tufts or loops of yarn, such as in velvet or chenille fabrics. Pile usually has a direction that can be determined by running the hand along the fabric in each direction and assessing the degree of resistance offered. *See also* Nap

PILLING The effect created by the entangling of surface fibres during washing, cleaning or wear and tear, which causes small 'balls' or 'bobbles' to appear on the surface of a fabric. It is generally not a problem with cotton or wool flat-weave fabrics and more likely to appear in polyester or knitted fabrics.

PLISSÉ A French term meaning pleated that is used to describe fabrics with a puckered or crinkled appearance.

PRE-SHRUNK Fabric that has been treated during processing to significantly reduce the amount of residual shrinkage in the finished fabric. This may be done by mechanical means, for example, Sanforising or compressive shrinkage, or with chemicals (such as resin stabilisation). It is important to note that there will still be a degree of shrinkage although this will be considerably reduced. *See also* Dimensional stability, Shrinkage, Sanforised, Residual shrinkage

PRINTING The process of applying colour to a fabric to produce a pattern. Printed fabrics have been made from earliest times and right up until the 19th century were produced exclusively with wooden blocks, stencils (or were hand painted). The advent of copper roller printing, allowed the reproduction of more complex and finely engraved designs on an industrial scale. These were subsequently largely superseded by flatbed and more recently rotary screen printing. Whilst the methods have changed over the years the basic principle has remained the same. The design is 'built up' on the cloth by printing individual colours, each requiring its own block, roller or screen to produce the complete pattern in repeat.

QUALITY The features or characteristics of a product or service that affect its ability to satisfy implied or stated needs. Commonly it expresses the concept of 'high' quality. The term is also used to categorise fabric in terms of its fibre content, construction, weight, finish and so on.

REPP A plain-weave fabric with a pronounced horizontal (weft-way) rib created by the use of alternating coarse and fine warp and weft yarns.

RESIDUAL SHRINKAGE The latent potential shrinkage in a fabric after processing is completed. This is the amount the fabric is likely to shrink in subsequent washing or cleaning andit varies considerably depending on the fibre content, weight, construction and finish of a fabric. For practical purposes most furnishing fabrics are in a range between 2 percent for printed cottons or poly/cottons up to 7-8 percent for heavy linen unions. Shrinkage is normally less in dry cleaning than in washing. *See also* Dimensional stability, Pre-shrunk, Sanforised, Shrinkage

REVERSIBLE A fabric that can be used on either side.

SANFORISED A mechanical compressive process that reduces residual shrinkage in fabrics.

SCOURED Fabrics, usually cotton, linen or linen unions that are washed in aqueous solutions to remove natural oils, starches and impurities instead of the stronger enzyme or chemical solvents that are used in bleaching or dyeing. The resultant fabric has a natural look and may still contain some cotton seeds and other imperfections that would be removed by bleaching. *See also* Bleaching

SCREEN PRINTING A process developed originally from stencilling in which a colourant is forced through unblocked areas of a mesh onto the fabric beneath. The mesh may be a fine woven silk or synthetic fabric on flat screens or a metal mesh on rotary (cylindrical) screens. In flatbed printing, the colourant is forced through the mesh by a squeegee or blade that traverses the stationary screen. With rotary printing the screen rotates and the squeegee remains stationary.

SEERSUCKER A fabric with characteristic alternating flat and puckered areas, usually in vertical stripes and produced in a number of different ways. Commonly the fabric is woven with warp yarns under varying tension or by using yarns with different shrinkage properties.

SELVAGE/SELVEDGE The two outer vertical edges of a fabric that are formed during weaving. They are invariably of different weave construction from the body of the fabric and their main purpose is to give strength to the edges of the fabric especially during processing, and to prevent fraying.

SHOT EFFECT An iridescent colour effect in a fabric produced by weaving a warp of one colour and a weft of strongly contrasting colour, for example, blue/orange, red/green. This effect is most pronounced in silk or silk-type fabrics.

SHRINKAGE Reduction in length or width of a fabric, caused usually by washing or dry cleaning although certain sensitive fabrics can shrink through changes in atmospheric humidity or heat.

SHRINK RESISTANT Fabrics that have a degree of dimensional stability that conforms to specified standards as a result of mechanical or chemical processing. It does not mean that the fabric will not shrink at all. *See also* Dimensional stability, Preshrunk, Residual shrinkage, Sanforised

SILK The fibre, yarn or fabric produced from the natural protein secretion of the silk moth larva that is unreeled as a continuous filament from the cocoons. *See also* Fibre, Filament yarn

SKEW A fabric condition in which the warp and weft, although perfectly straight, are not at right angles to each other.

SLUB A thicker section in a yarn. Occurring frequently in natural fibre products such as cotton, linen and silk, this effect is usually taken as a characteristic of the appearance of such fabrics, but excessive slubbiness may be judged to be a defect. Slubs are also used for special effects in certain fancy yarns.

SOIL RESIST/ SOIL RELEASE A finish such as Scotchguard that is applied to fabrics to inhibit staining/soiling of the surface and/or to facilitate its removal in washing or dry cleaning.

SPINNING The process of converting textile fibres into yarns. Staple fibres such as wool or cotton are drawn out and twisted in much the same way as was traditionally carried out on a spinning wheel, although nowadays the process is highly mechanised and extremely fast. Man-made filament yarns are spun from a fibre-forming substance that is forced in its molten state through 'spinnerets' that mimic the process whereby silk worms extrude their filaments through their glands.

STAPLE LENGTH The length of a textile fibre, it varies enormously from less than 2.5 centimetres (1 inch) for short-staple cotton, through coarse wool varieties of up to 40 centimetres (16 inches) and on to the continuous filament yarns of silk, which can be as much as 1,200 metres from a single cocoon, and man-made fibres whose length is effectively unlimited.

STRIKE OFF To produce colour samples of printed designs in order to assess for example, colour balance, correctness and appropriate interpretation of engraving prior to commercial production. The sample produced by this process, sometimes known as a Fent.

THREAD A term synonymous with 'yarn' in general. *See also* Yarn

UNION A fabric made with a warp of one kind of fibre and the weft of another. *See also* Linen Union

VAT DYE *See* Dyes

WARP Warp yarns (or ends) run vertically along the length of a woven fabric. *See also* Weft

WEFT Weft yarns (or picks) run horizontally across the width of a woven fabric. *See also* Warp

WOOL The fleece of the sheep that is processed to form woollen yarns. A proteinaceous fibre, it is resilient, soft and warm an owing to the physical make-up of the individual fibres, can be processed in a wide variety of ways to produce an infinite range of different finishes. *See also* Fibres *and* Wool, Glossary 1

WORSTED A wool fabric in which the yarns have been spun from combed wool in contrast to wool fabrics where the yarns are spun from carded wool.

YARN Textile fibres are spun or extruded to produce yarns, the basis of all woven textiles.
See also Fibre, Spinning

ACKNOWLEDGMENTS

Chris Halsey

Most of the content of this book has only been made possible by a long and tortuous learning process. My thanks go to the designers, weavers, printers, engravers, colourists and many others who have shared their wisdom and professional experience. Sadly, over the last 30 or 40 years the textile industry in the UK and Europe has declined.

In the 1970s there were at least six or seven excellent printworks in the UK; now there are barely two who can undertake top quality work. So from the early days my thanks go to the technicians at Standfast Printers and Stead McAlpin in the UK, particularly to Tony Sandiford and Alan Porthouse; Heberlein in Switzerland, Texunion in France and Pausa in Germany. Their colourists, printers and technicians were amongst the best in the world. More recently Federico Curti and Anna Salzano at Stamperia di Cassina Rizzardi have provided invaluable help, particularly in the field of digital printing.

No printer can do an excellent job if his screens are not of the highest quality, both from a technical and from a design interpretation point of view. And for this my grateful thanks go to Josep Mitats in Spain whose separation and engraving studio has produced fantastic work for us for over 30 years.

Amongst the most innovative and inspiring weaving mills I would single out Enzo and Mary Angiuoni, Riccardo Biagioni, Federico Spinelli, Ivan Vandekerckhove, Rudi Delchambre, Klaus Rohleder and Didier Benaud, for their inspirational design and technical innovation.

No list of acknowledgements would be complete without the inclusion of my many friends and associates in India, whose ability to create the most wonderful cotton and silk textiles is legendary: Ajit Kumar, my friend and dynamic weave supplier; Aditya and Vikram Jaipuria; Nagendrasa Kabadi and all their staff and technicians

And last but not least the many wonderful colleagues, too numerous to mention, who have supported me along the way, but in particular Tony Hennessy, Tanja Sharp and Allison Mackenzie, without their humour my journey might have been a much more bumpy road! And, of course, my dear friend and inspirational mentor Tricia Guild, without whom none of this would have been possible.

Wilhelmine van Aerssen

Every complaint can be considered free advice. Over the years, the number of complaints about fabrics that I received from retailers and consumers, has increased. This increase, I found out, was mainly due to an overall decline in knowledge and skill, when it became no longer necessary to be specifically qualified to sell fabrics. Knowledge prevents most of the complaints, so essentially, these preventable complaints triggered me to write this book.

I was glad to be joined by my friend Chris Halsey, who provided the technical information essential for anyone who deals with fabrics. Chris just retired after an almost lifelong career as technical director at Designers Guild and working together with him on this book was a great joy.

Designers Guild was the first brand that I started to represent in the Netherlands, 35 years ago. From the very beginning, Tricia Guild has been and will be my inspiration and shining example. Her views on colour, texture, design and style remain unprecedented. The collections by Ralph Lauren and Christian Lacroix complement the collections in a wonderful way.

Nobilis followed, where Denis Halard became my ever sympathetic and humorous professor of French history, culture and tradition, also present in their fabric designs and production methods. Coralie Halard offered me a refreshing view on the endless possibilities of presentation and decoration, and their son, Norman Halard, continues the Nobilis tradition.

Next, I started representing Osborne and Little. Together with Anthony Little, Peter Osborne created a brand that originates in and still breathes the swinging sixties. His specific taste has guaranteed beautiful fabric collections that have inspired me greatly.

Nina Campbell, whose style, elegance and tremendous sense of humour have always been a great example for me; Matthew Williamson, with his hip, extravagant designs that form a daring addition to all other collections; and Manuel Canovas with his rich and opulent Lorca designs. Laura and Barbara Osório add a wonderful mediterranean touch with their brand Pedroso & Osório.

Last but not least I want to mention William Yeoward, who became my guru in making life stylish yet at the same time easy and comfortable.

These beautiful brands, their designers and all other people behind their unique fabrics have inspired me and have taught me what I know today. Without them, this book would not have been written, so I want to thank all of them from the bottom of my heart.

There are some people who I want to thank specifically because they have been very important at some point during the 'making of' this book.

First I would like to thank Hélène Lesger, publisher and friend. Five years ago as a result of our many conversations about fabrics and interior decorating we sat together to write down our first concept. And now our dream has become a real and beautiful book. Without Hélène's continuing support and knowledge Chris and I would not have been able to get this work done.

And in alphabetical order many thanks to:
- Amanda Back, for all her support and backing behind the scenes
- Bernard Béchu, for his technical knowledge
- Chris Grafham, for his friendship and for being my all-round mentor
- Thérèse van der Lely and Peter Kooijman for their brilliant photography
- Graham Noakes, for his flamboyant presentations
- Hellen van der Valk, my friend and teacher
- Thomas Zoetman, for making a first overview of the various kinds of fabrics

I would also like to thank my team at Wilhelmine van Aerssen Agenturen B.V. Their support and loyalty during 35 years has been quintessential.

And, last but not least, I want to thank all our past, present and future customers.

BIBLIOGRAPHY

The Book of Silk, Philippa Scott (Thames & Hudson, 1993)

Textielwarenkast. Grondstoffen voor textiel gisteren, vandaag en morgen, Simone de Waart (Audax Textielmuseum Tilburg, 2011)

Textiel ABC (VTWS en ETITEX, 1979)

De Slaapkamer, Barbara & René Stoeltie (Terra Lannoo, 2003)

Fabric Magic, Melanie Payne (Frances Lincoln, 1987)

Pattern, Tricia Guild (Terra Lannoo, 2006)

Interior design of the 20th century, Anne Massey, World of Art series (Thames & Hudson, 1990)

Mary Gilliatt's Period Decorating, Mary Gilliatt (Conran Octopus, 1992)

Mauve, Simon Garfield (Faber and Faber, 2000)

Period-Style Soft Furnishings, Judith Miller (Mitchell Beazley, 1996)

The Soft Furnishings Book, Terence Conran (Conran Octopus, 1991)

The Complete Upholsterer. A Practical Guide to Upholstering Traditional Furniture, Carole Thomerson (Frances Lincoln, 1989)

The Style Source Book, Judith Miller (Mitchell Beazley, 1998)

Toile de Jouy. Printed Textiles in the classic French Style, Mélanie Riffel, Sophie Rouart, Marc Walter (Thames and Hudson, 2003)

PICTURE CREDITS